Promoting

FRIENDSHIPS

in the Playground

A Lucky Duck Book

Promoting

FRIENDSHIPS

in the Playground

A Peer Befriending Programme for Primary Schools

Brigette Bishop

P·C·P

Paul Chapman
Publishing

Paul Chapman Publishing
A SAGE Publications Company
1 Oliver's Yard
55 City Road
London EC1Y 1SP

SAGE Publications Inc.
2455 Teller Road
Thousand Oaks, California 91320

SAGE Publications India Pvt Ltd.
B-42, Panchsheel Enclave
Post Box 4109
New Delhi 110 017

Commissioning Editors: George Robinson
Editorial Team: Mel Maines, Sarah Lynch, Wendy Ogden.
Designer: Nick Shearn
Illustrator: Philippa Drakeford

A catalogue record for this book is available from the British Library

Library of Congress Control Number 2006904348

ISBN13 978-1-4129-1078-1
ISBN10 1-4129-1078-1 (pbk)

Printed on paper from sustainable resources

Printed in Great Britain by The Cromwell Press Ltd, Trowbridge, Wiltshire

Contents

Acknowledgements

> Anyone who will not receive the Kingdom of God like a little child will never enter it. (Mark 10v15)

As adults we often lose touch with the simplicity of childish ways and conversely it is to the very ones that I set out to help that I owe my thanks for all they have taught me. It is my hope that the simplicity of this scheme – children helping other children – is not lost in my attempts to promote it.

Special thanks to:

> the colleagues with whom I have worked over the years both in mainstream drama and modern language teaching and latterly in the field of Behaviour Support

> my long-suffering husband.

The Programme for Pupils

The programme that is used with both the children and supervisors throughout this book is referred to as Playground Pals.

This was the original title of the book and though it was a very snappy title it was felt that it didn't describe the purpose of the book. We did feel it important that the programme for participants did have a catchy title to be used to promote it in the school and we decided that Playground Pals was ideal.

We do hope that you and the participants enjoy the programme.

How to use the CD-ROM

The CD-ROM contains a PDF file, labelled 'Activity sheets.pdf' which consists of all the activity sheets in this resource. You will need Acrobat Reader version 3 or higher to view and print these resources.

To photocopy the activity sheets directly from this book, set your photocopier to enlarge by 125% and align the edge of the page to be copied against the leading edge of the copier glass (usually indicated by an arrow).

Introduction

There were several reasons for deciding to write this book. The main reason: to develop a scheme that would improve the quality of playtime for children and staff. This is in response to a need that I had seen in schools.

The following factors underpinned my writing:

▸ I am currently employed as a member of a Behaviour Support Team, part of whose role is to support schools in dealing with pupils presenting problematic behaviour. A significant part of my working day is devoted to attempting to sort out children's behaviour problems, many of which occur in the playground. It was during my observations of playtimes that I became increasingly aware that many of the problems stemmed from some of the children's poor social skills, which manifested in an inability to play and often resulted in conflict.

▸ Often, when observing a child in the playground, I would notice the loners, the friendless, the bullies and the bullied. When talking to the children about playtime they confirmed these observations by complaining of name-calling, bullying, lack of space, lack of friends and fights caused by football.

▸ Through observation and conversations with children and staff, it appeared that a lack of structured play (for example, games) and the ensuing boredom also contributed to disputes.

▸ I saw a need for some form of supervision other than that of the teacher or lunch-time supervisor, who do not have time to play with the children. There should be someone to provide low-level intervention by involving children in play with peers, mediating, modelling appropriate social skills or helping to resolve conflict.

▸ Having 'done' playground duty as a mainstream teacher, I know how tiresome it can be to be bombarded by an endless stream of tales of woe and problems in your ten-minute coffee break, usually because the children want attention or lack the appropriate social skills to play properly and sort out minor conflicts. How helpful it would be if there could be a trained team of helper children who could intervene initially and play with those experiencing problems. This would also, hopefully, reduce the amount of time during lessons that teachers have to use when dealing with playground problems.

▸ I am a great believer in children helping children and would often notice older children 'mothering' or 'fathering' younger ones. A colleague has trained students in the six-form in basic counselling skills for use as a method of intervention with pupils experiencing problems at secondary school level. As a classroom practitioner, I often used a pairing system to help a weaker pupil socially or academically.

▸ While developing the scheme and analysing its effectiveness, I realised that, for long lasting effective change, the various interacting strands of the playground need to be considered, such as:

the quality and appearance of the physical space the children play on

the views of the wider school community such as parents, carers and governors

the views of the children and staff.

In line with my initial observations and conversations, this book is predominantly for the children, as I still believe that will have the greatest impact on the playground and school environment. However, as the quality of lunch-time supervision seemed to be the next most needy area to impact the school system, I developed a four week training session for lunch-time supervisors designed to complement and run alongside the Pal's training. There are also working examples of how this can be further developed within the context of whole-staff meetings and playground policy. I also include examples of surveys for teachers, pupils, governors and parents in the appendices to help facilitate a needs analysis with regards to the playground should you wish to fit Playground Pals into an on-going action plan of playground policy.

The national context and related research

The three areas that form the backbone to the scheme are:

1. Pupils helping each other (peer support).
2. Developing social skills (social competence).
3. Playground games.

It is thus under these three headings that I catalogue the national context. It is interesting to note that over the five years I have taken to develop this scheme, much more has subsequently been published on peer support schemes. This resurgence of interest in peer relations as a strategy to solve some of the social and emotional problems experienced by children at school is reflected in the national context.

Peer support and breaktime

The playground was identified in national studies by the DfES Bullying, Don't Suffer in Silence (2000) as the place where three quarters of bullying behaviour takes place in primary schools. The same report suggests methods to help combat bullying, one of which is peer counselling. Key findings from a later DfES study into children's perspectives on bullying (2003) reveal that the three most helpful factors in helping pupils to deal with bullying are:

1. Friendships.
2. Avoidance strategies.
3. Learning to stand up for yourself.

The same study reveals 'name-calling' as the most popular form of bullying. Recommendations from the study advocate a child-centred approach and that more attention be given to the role of friendships to combat bullying, quoting the 'buddy' system as one means of facilitating friendships.

This idea of a 'buddy' providing a scaffold to help children progress across the next step of their development derives from Vygotsky's (1978) work and is alluded to in much subsequent writing on child development. Scroufe, Cooper, DeHart (1988), Pollard (1996), and Smith, Cowie (1996).

Cowie and Sharp (1996) state that:

> ◄ Peer support begins with the natural willingness of most young people to act in a cooperative, friendly way towards another. ◄

They conclude that peer support systems build on this quality and provide a structure that promotes the individual's potential for responsibility and caring.

The Mental Health Foundation and ChildLine founded the Peer Support Forum in 1998. Its purpose is to coordinate the widely developing work of peer support. In 1999, it outlined Principles of Good Practice in Peer Support Projects. The key principles that relate to this scheme are:

▸ Young people are central to the project.

▸ Young people are provided with the skills to support each other more effectively.

▸ The self-esteem of young people is promoted.

▸ Clear objectives, boundaries and ground rules are established for all aspects of the project, after discussion and agreement with the young people involved.

▸ Young people receive appropriate and ongoing training.

An evaluation of seven peer support projects (including a playground listening service) funded by the Mental Health Foundation reported significant benefits to the pupils, such as increased self-confidence, communication skills and emotional development. Some of the positive impacts on the schools were a reduction in pupil stress and bullying and improved interpersonal skills amongst the pupils (Peer Support Report 2002).

Pellegrini's and Blatchford article (2002) highlights the importance of 'key players' who have a vital role in the development of friendships and games. They conclude that these 'leadership skills probably attract other children and leaders gain additional skills to boost their social competence by practising and learning their social skills.' The same article suggests that success on the playground can help with adjustment to school academic ability and self-esteem.

Social competence and breaktime

The significance of breaktimes as a mechanism for children to develop social competence is highlighted in much of Peter Blatchford's work.

Results from a recent national survey of breaktimes in primary and secondary schools (Blatchford and Sumpner, 1998) indicate that the most frequently occurring problem at both primary and secondary levels 'was the poor behaviour of a small number of pupils who have difficulties in socialising'. Where behaviour had improved, it was due to the fact 'that pupils engaged in better quality breaktime activities'. Telephone follow-ups 'indicated that school intervention and policies at breaktime could contribute to improvements'.

There is an allied view that children are required to demonstrate higher levels of social competence during relatively unstructured times such as breaktime. (Pellegrini and Blatchford (2000).) The minimal adult presence requires children to develop social skills such as turn-taking, sharing, conflict resolution and negotiation in order to survive successfully. More recently, where unsupervised play time has been diminished by the knock on effects of increased numbers of single parents, working mothers, perceived dangers to children, more after school clubs, increased television viewing and computer games, the school playground is perhaps one of the few areas where children have the opportunity to develop socially competent behaviour. It has been suggested that cutting breaktime to balance longer teaching hours due to curriculum demands and as a means of modifying inappropriate behaviour is not helpful for the development of social competence in pupils, and could be endorsing the very behaviour it seeks to correct. Barnes (1995) refers to Slukin's (1987) research that concludes that the playground, presenting a social microcosm of adult life, offers children an important preparation for that adult life. Could it be that these playtime skills provide the key to solving the increasing problem of anti-social behaviour so prevalent in society today?

Playground games and breaktime

The importance (and demise in recent years) of games at breaktime is obvious to the casual observer. They offer a safe structure in which children:

▸ can interact and start to get to know each other

▸ temporarily break up friendship and ethnic groups

▸ teach social skills such as turn-taking, following instructions, negotiation, team playing and offer a light-hearted release from the demands of the curriculum.

Pellegrini and Blatchford (2002) quote Bateson (1976) and state that:

> Games have an important role to the extent that they provide a familiar routine or scaffold around which unacquainted children can interact.

Their studies of the development of playground games and peer relations confirm that social relationships in school develop from these repeated interactions in games.

The training sessions

The four training sessions are intended to develop the following skills in the pupils, many of which they will model and hopefully teach other pupils:

understanding of the scheme and its aims

turn-taking

sharing

understanding of basic emotional responses

good listening

understanding others

understanding body language

eye contact

being friendly

being helpful

being encouraging

problem-solving

self-confidence

communication

anger management

assertiveness

self-awareness and other awareness

ability to praise and raise another's self-esteem

playground games.

The following teaching techniques are used to develop these skills:

games

rounds

drama

role-play

discussion.

Greater detail about these techniques and how to run the group can be found in the teacher's notes with each session and in the section 'Running the Training Sessions'.

Promoting Friendships in the Playground has been piloted and evaluated in primary schools in the London Borough of Bromley. Many schools have used it to contribute towards their bid for the National Healthy Schools Standard. It addresses many of the areas covered in Citizenship, PSHE and complements the Social and Emotional Aspects of Learning (SEAL) materials being introduced into primary schools as part of the National Strategy. In addition, it actively promotes key outcomes from the Every Child Matters Agenda: be healthy, enjoy and achieve and make a positive contribution.

It is my hope that the scheme will help create emotionally and mentally healthier playground climates by addressing some of the behaviour problems occurring in the playground.

The following outcomes are aimed for.

Pupils:

▸ Improved social skills and self-esteem of both pupils being helped on the playground and pupils helping, giving rise to improved relationships for a wider spectrum of pupils, which in turn will result in improved playtimes for the school community.

▸ Increased knowledge of playground games resulting in less boredom.

Staff:

▸ Improved behaviour management skills and self-esteem for LTSs.

▸ Improved communication between all staff.

▸ Reduction in stress experienced by staff on playground duty.

▸ Reduction in the amount of teacher time spent on following up playground incidents.

How to Use the Materials

There are slight variations for the Year 6 and the Year 2 programme depending on whether you want to train juniors or infants, but they follow the same structure.

Gathering data

Before implementing the scheme you could collect information about the community's views about breaktimes. The Appendix provides some surveys for parents, carers, teachers, pupils and supervisors.

Informing pupils about the scheme

If a survey was conducted the results could be given in an assembly and the pupils told about the proposal to have trained Year 6 (or Year 2) pupils on duty at playtimes to help make breaktimes happier for everybody. Posters and how pupils can apply to be a Pal are in the Appendix.

Selecting the Pals

I have found it useful to spend ten minutes with Year 6 prior to the first session to explain the aims of the course. It may be useful for the teacher and class to draw up a job specification for a Playground Pal to help focus the class on what skills they will need to develop. Further language work could be developed with letters of application and interviews conducted to select the first group. (See Appendix.) Alternatively, select a mixture of model pupils and those who may have some behaviour problems, but for whom the kudos of being a Pal would help to raise their self-esteem and improve their social skills. To begin with it is a good idea to have the majority of the Pals as your more 'ideal' candidates with two or three who may need the discipline and kudos of being a Pal. The boy/girl split should reflect the percentage in the year group if possible.

The first set of Pals will then introduce the scheme to the school by way of a whole-school assembly. Each time a new team is trained, the scheme could be highlighted again by way of an assembly.

Informing the parents and carers

It is important to have parental permission and support for the scheme. A draft letter for parents can be found in the Appendix. You may wish to ask for parents' views on breaktimes at the same time (also in the Appendix).

Informing staff including lunch-time supervisors

Discuss the scheme with the head and other members of staff. It is vital that it is endorsed and supported by the whole school. Many schools have included the scheme as part of their bid to obtain the National Healthy Schools Standard. Decide how you will select the first Pals and research the specific needs of the playground, for example, small playground, lack of playground games and bullying problems, so that you can adapt the sessions as necessary. I have included staff, pupil and parent/governor surveys in the Appendix should you wish to use them to help you gather information.

Lunch-time supervisors

Whether you choose to train the supervisors or not, they need to be informed about the scheme and told what the Pals will be dealing with and what they won't. This will vary from school to school, for example, Pals will not be expected to intervene with fighting children but will be intervening with children who have nobody to play with and so will hopefully reduce non-essential demands on supervisors' time. If you have enough Pals you may wish to use them in the dinner hall to help supervise.

Running the training schemes

(Mainly sourced from Bliss, Robinson and Maines (1995))

Circle Time provides an ideal technique to run the training sessions. Bliss et al (1995) suggest that the process of Circle Time helps develop:

▸ Self-awareness – self-knowledge, who I am.

▸ Personal skills – feelings and emotions.

▸ Group and social skills – relationships, knowing how I function in a group.

Self-awareness

Good group work promotes self-awareness – as we learn about ourselves, we also learn about and understand others. Activities that develop this are personal statements such as, 'I like...' and 'I feel...'

The rules of the group demand that the group give acceptance to their 'I' statements, therefore the message develops that it is safe to share personal thoughts and feelings.

Members of the group learn:

- to listen
- to avoid put downs and negative statements
- to respect confidentiality.

Self-disclosure

The unwritten rule about self-disclosure is to start it at a safe level, such as, 'One thing I like is...', 'I dislike...' moving onto more personal statements, such as, 'When I'm left out, I feel...'

Due to the nature of the training sessions, self-disclosure moves at a more rapid pace than I would normally ask from a group. Within Session 1, the children are asked to move from, 'One thing I like/dislike...' to, 'A time when I felt left out was..., it made me feel...'

Most groups have been fine with this, however, the option to pass is there if they wish.

The following aspects are therefore very important.

Being positive

Never ask children to name names or admit to misdemeanours. Concentrate on feelings.

'A time when I was left out was when (avoid name) my friend went off with (avoid name) someone else.'

If negatives arise try and turn them into positives.

'I'm not good at anything.' Ask the group to help, 'You're very good at being in a group,' 'You're a good listener.'

The pass rule

Children must always be allowed to pass. At the end of the round go back and give them the opportunity to make a comment. If they still choose to pass, your verbal and non-verbal message must be that passing is always acceptable. I find it useful to pass around an age appropriate item, such as a shell or a small toy, to signify who has the turn to speak.

Confidentiality

Always stress that the information given within the group is confidential (unless a disclosure is made). You can discuss with the pupils the reason for this.

Self-esteem

Self-esteem has been a focus in much of my work as a Behaviour Support Teacher. Pupils who have a positive view of themselves are more likely to achieve more, socially and academically, than those pupils whose self-esteem is low. Much of the focus of the training sessions is to raise the self-esteem of the pupils, so they, in turn, can raise the self-esteem of others.

Facilitator's skills

As the facilitator, we model that the group is about listening and acceptance. We have to create safety from ridicule, embarrassment and teasing. We also have to be prepared to deal with wind-ups.

Pupils may sometimes make comments that you feel the need to respond to, such as,

'I like to hurt my sister.' You can accept the statement and move onto the next pupil, or say, 'I haven't given you much time to think. I'll come back to you later.'

However tempting it may be, it is not appropriate to make comments such as, 'I can't agree with that,' or, 'That's silly.' The group is not an advice, sympathy or therapy group. Advice, sympathy and solutions have no place within the Circle so the following would not be acceptable:

'I know what you are saying, I felt the same when...' 'That's terrible, I think you were very brave.' 'Why don't you try...?' 'If that had happened to me, I'd have done...' We should never seek further details: 'And what happened then?' 'Who did that to make you feel...?'

We may get presented with information that is painful and we feel that we have to respond. Children might make comments like: 'I get sad when I don't see my dad.' 'I get sad when my mum shouts at my dad.'

It is best to accept and move on. A group process is under way and an understanding and acceptance of the feelings may be sufficient. The process is intended to help an individual to be aware of her feeling.

If a comment is made that you feel you must do something about you will need to do this privately. You could give the pupil a 'talking ticket' (a ticket sized piece of card or paper with the words 'talking ticket' written on it) as a sign that they can come and speak to you at break if they want to. You could use active listening skills that are based on feelings rather than facts. Do not interrogate. Provide the opportunity for the pupil to refuse to disclose if she wishes to remain silent.

An opening comment might be, 'You said in the group you were sad when... would you like to tell me more?' 'When you said... I thought you were feeling... would you like to talk about it?'

If you realise the child is making disclosures about abuse, then you must not ask questions at this time. Follow your school and authority procedures.

The sessions

Length

Each session lasts approximately 30 minutes. Suggestions for what can be left out if you are short of time are given. The follow-up session needs about 45 minutes.

You can run the training sessions in any fashion that is helpful to you, weekly or daily.

Adult participation

It is important that the designated teacher, who is to be responsible for the scheme, joins in all the sessions and contributes to the rounds etc. It is useful to have additional adult help, for example, an L.S.A. or classroom assistant, in as many sessions as possible, to help monitor the role-plays and pair work. It is important that any additional adult helpers are well-known to the group if they can only join you for one or two sessions, in order not to detract from any trust being built within the group. The success of the scheme depends upon regular teacher enthusiasm and input through supervision and refresher sessions.

Games

I've collated the many and varied games with brief descriptions. Where it says 'Children's Choice', you may like to practise some of the alternatives from the suggested list. You may wish to devote a separate session to games to allow extra time so that the Pals are completely familiar with them all and have a wider repertoire to choose from. Knowledge and experience of the games is one of the most important aspects of the Pal's training, as these provide the structure that will help promote the social skills and self-esteem of both the Pals and those they are helping.

Differentiating the sessions for Year 2

The full script for the sessions is given for Year 6. At the end of each session, additional notes provide the changes necessary for younger pupils. Additional activity sheets for the younger pupils are provided, if appropriate, after the

Year 2 notes, apart from changing the phrasing and some of the questions, the main difference is that a Year 2 group will need more time and will move at a slower pace. I have found role-play to be an effective method of enabling them to learn through experience, so more use is made of this technique. You may think it appropriate to modify the programme and add an extra session.

Implementing the scheme

Uniform

Various means have been used to make the Pals recognisable: sashes, sweatshirts in winter and T-shirts in summer showing a Playground Pals logo are just some. Most school budgets are tight, so only three or four are produced to cover the daily Pals. Caps are often decided against for hygiene reasons.

Equipment

Some schools have produced a box of skipping ropes, balls etc. for use with the Pals within a designated area of the playground. Children may come and borrow from the box and play within the area. It doesn't necessarily mean that the children who come up need the Pals to play with them, but it is a safe area for those who wish to play near or with a Pal. It is also useful to have a book where the Pals can note down anything they feel that a teacher should know about at the end of play. This can be kept in reception or the classroom and referred to during supervision sessions.

Support for selected children

A great problem-solver is assigning a Pal to an individual child as long as the Pal works with the child and some of her peer group, so that the Pal gradually becomes dispensable. You can also assign Pals to specific trouble spots around the school, for example, cloakrooms and toilets.

Support for Pals

The follow-up session is where the children can report back and problem-solve any difficulties that have arisen. This session is also used to pool and record ideas for the next training sessions, which the current Pals will run under supervision of a member of staff, thus perpetuating the Playground Pals. Evaluation of the scheme has shown that it is important that there are on-going supervision and refresher sessions for the Pals throughout the year, examples of which are included in the follow-up sessions. It is recommended that these supervision sessions take place half-termly.

Boundaries

It is important to stress that the children are not intended to replace the teacher or lunch-time supervisor and are not expected to intervene in a situation where they or another child may be at risk. It is up to the individual school to decide what constitutes a 'no go' area with regard to the Pals' intervention and this needs to be clearly communicated to all staff and pupils.

Pals should be able to identify children who may need their help, either because they have no friends or have fallen out with their friends and by employing basic befriending skills, identify the problem and help the child to solve it. This may involve the Pal setting a game up with some of the pupils peer group, modelling appropriate social skills, mediating between friends or leading a LTS or teacher to a particular problem.

Evaluation

After careful evaluation of the scheme, the following aspects are vital for its long-term success in a school:

▸ The commitment and role of the teacher. The success of the scheme will depend on the commitment of the staff. The workload may need to be shared. As well as organising the training they will have to produce duty rotas, provide on-going support for the Pals and liaise with other members of staff.

▸ The training sessions for the second group of Pals needs to follow-on quite quickly to keep the impetus going and to ensure that the first set of Pals do not get bored, disillusioned or burnt out.

▸ The assemblies, particularly the first, need to create a high profile for the Pals within the school and set the standard for expected behaviour with regard to them. If necessary, some rules can be drawn up.

▸ It is helpful if the Pals and training of LTSs is part of an on-going playground policy that takes account of the other factors which contribute to the playground, for example, space and involvement of the wider school community. Evaluation from the Pals is usually positive.

What the children say

The following are a range of comments taken from follow-up sessions in schools:

I enjoy teaching little children games.

I enjoy being able to help people.

I enjoy making little ones happy.

I enjoy children looking up to me.

The kids have calmed down!

I enjoy knowing more children.

I never lost my temper when the little kids called me names.

I've got more confidence.

Playtime is more fun now.

It makes you feel good having some responsibility.

Preparing next year's Pals

It is a good idea to use existing Pals to help train the next year's Pals. The second half of the summer term is usually a good time. Choose four to six who can join in the sessions and give input as and when required. You could also pair up a new and an old Pal to send out together for the first couple of sessions. In the September you can have a preliminary run through of the reminder pack prior to sending the Pals out and then train some more after the follow-up session.

Session 1: Pals' Training Year 6

Before commencing the training you will have considered:

▸ Discussing the scheme with staff, parents, carers and young people.

▸ Surveying current opinions about playtimes.

▸ Explaining the scheme to all the pupils.

▸ Advertising for volunteer Pals.

▸ Selecting the Pals.

▸ Selecting appropriate uniforms for Pals.

▸ Identifying staff to train and support Pals.

▸ Whether training supervisors is appropriate.

Aims

To break down barriers and inhibitions within the group.

To help the group appreciate the feelings of those with whom they will be working.

To develop listening skills and show the importance of listening.

To establish a safe working framework for the group through rule making.

To help the group to be aware of different types of body language.

Resources

Our Rules activity sheet.

Playground Observation activity sheet.

Teacher's notes

It is important for the group to sit in a circle, if possible on chairs. If no chairs are available, it is important that any adults involved in the group also sit on the floor. This is to reinforce the unity and equality of everyone in the group and helps the children to feel important and valued, which will give them more confidence to speak.

Introduction

Thank the children for agreeing to train to be a Pal. Remind them of their roles and explain the purpose of their training.

Name games

The idea behind the first two games is to give everyone in the group a chance to practise speaking aloud in front of the whole group by saying something that is easy and familiar. This prepares the pupils for the later rounds where they will be asked to speak about their feelings. Both games need to be quite fast moving to keep the momentum going. For 'Harry calling Sally', I usually select two children and model for the group before we start playing. It is helpful to ask the children to have something ready to say for both these games.

Rules

It may be helpful if you have a particularly lively group to write the rules out and put them up for all to see each time you run the group. You could photocopy Our Rules Sheet onto card, if you wished to use them. It is important to elicit the rules from the group, as this encourages ownership; even if you want to use the suggested rules, do this by phrasing their suggestions in such a way so as to concur with the rules. Often the children tend to phrase rules negatively, i.e. 'Don't...' Ask them to phrase the rules that you decide to use positively. It is important to receive all their suggestions with acceptance and try to incorporate them all. For example, a child suggests no fighting or kicking; your reply could be, 'Would that be included in the rule, 'There are no put downs (verbal or physical)?'

Listening games

The listening game is intended to be a light-hearted look at listening skills. It is helpful if you are able to model it first for the pupils as it provides a concrete example for them to analyse. Choose a volunteer who will talk to you about their hobbies, for example. Explain that whatever you do they are not to stop talking. You can fidget, yawn, interrupt, look away... have fun with it! You can then ask the children, 'How did you know I wasn't listening?' Likewise, modelling good listening skills with a volunteer – eye contact, nodding head, appropriate questions – is also useful for them. I find the phrase, 'Stop and swap' useful for getting the children to swap roles quickly. For the rounds you may need to provide them with some words such as sad, happy, lonely and wanted. Time permitting I often include a round, for example, 'Someone who listens to me is...' This is particularly good if you are dealing with a group of children who may not have anyone who listens to them and you could set up paired listening opportunities at other times.

A space on my right

This section is intended to help the children understand what it feels like to be left out. If nobody has been left out during the game, explain that this is good, but ask how the problem could be solved if some children had not been chosen. The idea is for the group to suggest a way to identify when someone has been chosen, for example, fold your arms. If there are inappropriate suggestions such as put your hand up, discuss why, for example, your arm will ache if it is up for a long time.

Rounds

It is important to remind the group that it is OK to pass on a round. Your attitude as facilitator should always be that it is acceptable to pass. At the end of the round go back and ask those who passed if they would now like to contribute.

Stories and discussion

The idea is to help the group to identify the sort of children who may need their help and to develop their understanding of body language and different emotional responses. If they don't come up with any examples, provide them with some. You can also use pictures to discuss body language: storybooks or comics are often good material.

Discussion

Due to time restraints, I usually just pose the questions and the children put their hands up if they want to contribute. You may prefer to pair or group them up to discuss the questions and get them to report back, if you have time. Some facts to consider when deciding how the Pals will be recognised:

▸ Some schools have found that sweatshirts need to be big enough to go over coats in winter and may need to be replaced by T-shirts in the heat of the summer and that these are neither practical nor cost effective.

▸ Some schools use bands or bibs in a striking colour, with or without the addition of a pupil identity badge and photo.

Preparation for Playground Observation session

Hand out the activity sheet. Pair up those pupils who may find this task difficult. Pupils only need to do one playground observation and could be provided with a clipboard to facilitate writing and sketching. They do not need to answer all the questions.

Reflection

I have found it useful to note down the skills from each section so as to remind the children at the beginning of the next session and use for a future reminder.

Zip Zap

If you are short on time, leave out Zip Zap and the reflection round. You could begin Session 2 with a round, 'Something I learnt from Session 1 was...' Zip Zap can be played in a session where it says Children's Choice. You may also wish to briefly run through the discussion points and send the pupils away to think about how they would like to be recognised and feed this back at another time.

Activities

Name games

My name is and this is...

The teacher models how to play this by introducing themselves and the person on their right, who in turn introduces themselves and the person on their right and so on around the circle.

Sally calling Harry, Harry calling Mike

An excellent game for mixing up friends sitting together. Everyone stands. The facilitator models the game by walking towards a pupil to take his or her place in the circle, for example Sally, and says, 'Miss/Mr... calling Sally', at which point Sally must quickly choose another child and repeat the phrase, 'Sally calling...' whilst walking towards the child to take his or her place and so on. This needs to be quite fast moving and to make it even faster, two children can be calling names at the same time!

Rules

Introduce the talking object (see Running the sessions) and use some sentence completion rounds, for example, 'How I like to be treated in a group...'

Explain that it is necessary to create some rules to ensure that everyone feels safe and happy in the group. Brainstorm and elicit rules from the group by well chosen questions such as:

- Bearing in mind the statements made in the rounds, what rules shall we have to help everyone feel safe and relaxed?
- Why should we keep what is said in this group private?
- How can we show respect for each other?

Explain that you do not think anyone will break a rule, but if they do they will have one warning, if they break a rule a second time, they will spend one minute outside the circle.

(I have only ever had to give a warning once.)

Do not assume that a group already familiar with Circle Time strategies will respond more positively to the sessions than a group who is not, as group dynamics will alter with the situation.

Some suggested rules are:

- We listen when someone else is speaking.
- We may pass.
- What we say in the group stays within the group.
- There are no put downs, only put ups!

Listening games

Not listening

Ask for a volunteer to sit in the middle of the circle with you. Ask them to tell you what they like to do in their spare time, explain that it is important that they keep talking and not be put off by whatever you do. While the volunteer talks, fidget, avoid eye contact, look around the room, interrupt with irrelevant information about yourself. The idea is to model non-listening behaviour and have fun with it!

Ask the group to describe one non-listening behaviour. They can then act this out:

- Put the pupils into pairs – A and B.

- A's start by telling B's what they like to do out of school, B's do not listen. A's and B's then swap roles. (Allow about two minutes for each conversation.)

- Back in the group discuss how it feels not to be listened to or, if time is short, go around the circle allowing each child the opportunity to complete the sentence, 'When I'm not listened to I feel...'

- Model listening behaviour with a volunteer and then discuss.

- Repeat the previous game, this time each partner takes a turn demonstrating listening behaviour.

- Use the round:

When I'm listened to I feel...

Ask the group, 'Why are good listening skills essential for a Pal?'

Answers could be to help the children feel that they matter, to show that you are really interested in what they have to say and in helping them.

A space on my right

There is a space on my right and I would like X to sit in it.

- The teacher models the game by choosing a child to sit on the empty chair on her right saying, 'There's a space on my right and I'd like X to sit in it.'

- X moves to sit in the empty seat, make's eye contact with the teacher and says, 'Thank you.'

- The child with the empty chair on their right now has a turn, and so on.

- Stop the game after two minutes. Ask who has not been chosen. Who has been chosen once? Twice?

- Get the group to identify the problem that some children will be chosen several times whilst others may not be chosen at all. Ask for suggestions to problem-solve this and ensure that no one else is left out. One possible solution is for a child to fold his arms when he has been chosen. The children then only choose someone who has not got folded arms.

Sami

Sami doesn't have any brothers and sisters.

No other children to play with at home (sad).

His parents spoil him (yes – thumbs up).

He is used to having his own way (I always get my own way).

On the playground he likes to be 'Boss' (I'm in charge) in any games the children are playing.

He likes to play his way and to his rules, whether or not they are the proper rules. If it was a game like It, he would never want to be 'It', if it was a game like Farmer's in the Den, he would always have to be the Farmer.

If anyone tries to stand up to him, he runs off and cries (turn around and pretend to cry).

The other children don't like playing with him.

He doesn't understand why he hasn't got any friends (shrug shoulders).

Sasha

Sasha is new to the school (look shy).

She started halfway through the term when all the rest of her class had already made friends.

She was bullied at her last school (look scared) and hasn't got a lot of confidence (look down) and is very shy (I'm very shy).

She hasn't made any friends.

She sits on the seat by herself at playtimes (I'm all alone) or follows the teacher or lunch-time supervisor around (I feel safe with you).

Questions to prompt discussion

▸ Have they ever felt like these children?

▸ Have they seen children acting like this on the playground?

▸ What is body language? What different types of body language might they see on the playground? What body language might the children in the story have shown?

Ask for volunteers to mime different emotions: angry, sad, lonely, happy etc., or, in pairs, get the children to mould their partner into a statue for the rest of the group to guess what emotion they represent.

Explain that boys often show they are upset by acting out aggressive behaviour, whereas girls often withdraw when they are upset. Ask for any examples or exceptions that they may have observed.

The children often become amateur psychologists at this point and provide wonderful examples and exceptions from their own experience!

Revision

Revise the aims of being a Playground Pal. Discuss what the Pals will wear to be recognised. This is important to sort out early as sweatshirts, T-shirts and sashes may need to be ordered.

Playground observation

This is to research what is happening on the playground. Hand out the activity sheet. Pair up those pupils who may find the writing difficult and explain the task.

Zip Zap

Again the facilitator models this by choosing a child to Zip. With hands together as if praying, you point your hands at the child and say, 'Zip X.' It is now X's turn to 'Zip' someone else.

▸ After a few goes, the teacher introduces Zap. If someone Zips you, you can put both hands up in front of your face and deflect the Zip by saying, 'Zap.'

▸ The person now has to choose someone else to Zip.

▸ The rules are (usually!) that if someone is trying to Zip, they can only be Zapped once; after that someone has to accept their Zip.

▸ This is a frantic, fun game to close with which the children love. If you wish you may discuss how the way this is played relates to what you have discussed this session. I usually find the children are good at making sure everyone is chosen.

Reflection

What skills have we learnt from this session?

Listening, empathy, awareness of body language.

Our Rules

We may pass.

....

There are no put downs, only put ups.

....

We listen.

....

What we say stays here.

Playground Observation

Use the following questions to help you with your observation.

Don't worry if you can't answer them all.

1. What games are being played on the playground?

    _____

    _____

    _____

2.   Are there any children with nobody to play with? What are they doing?

    _____

    _____

    _____

3. Are they feeling happy or sad? Why do you think they are feeling this way?

    _____

    _____

    _____

4. What other things are happening on the playground?

    _____

    _____

    _____

5. What difficulties do you see children having on the playground?

    _____

    _____

    _____

6. What is going well on the playground?

    _____

    _____

    _____

Differentiation Guidelines Year 2

Games

Sally calling Harry, Harry calling Mike

In my experience Year 2 children can't choose who they want to call fast enough to make this game as fast paced as it needs to be. One way of limiting their choice and thus making it quicker, is to get children to fold their arms when they have been chosen, the person calling is then limited to those with unfolded arms. Generally, I have found that games with minimal choice options seem to work best for a Year 2 group, so you may even replace this with another game whereby the children take it in turns to say their name and their favourite animal.

Rules

It is better, I think, to show the Year 2s some suggested rules. Explain that the rules are needed for everyone to feel safe and happy in the group. Discuss with them what they mean and why they think they are important. Ask if anyone has any other suggestions, these can usually be incorporated into the existing rules.

Listening games

Perhaps ask them to tell you what their favourite TV programmes are.

Discussion about stories

Questions to ask:

'How would we know that Sami and Sasha were upset if they were on our playground?'

'What would they look like?'

'How do we use our bodies to show that we are upset, lonely or sad?'

Ask for volunteers to mime different emotions: angry, sad, lonely, happy, excited, worried…

Explain that using our bodies to show how we feel is known as body language, looking at someone's body language on the playground can help us to understand how they are feeling. Discuss the fact that boys often show they are upset by acting out aggressive behaviour, whereas girls often withdraw when they are upset. Ask for any examples or exceptions that they may have observed. The children often become amateur psychologists at this point and provide wonderful examples and exceptions from their own experience.

Revise aims of being a Playground Pal. Discuss how Pals will be recognised, by wearing a sweatshirt, cap, sash, etc. This is important to sort out early as sweatshirts may need to be ordered.

Preparation for next session

Research what is happening on the playground. Hand out the activity sheet. Pair up those pupils who may find it difficult to do the reading and writing, or suggest that they draw the answers.

Game

Zip Zap or Cowboy, Freeze! (p47) are quite good games to end with.

Reflection round

'Something that I learnt from this session is...'

Playground Observation

Use pictures and sentences to show what is happening on the playground.

Happy children are…

_____

_____

_____

_____

Sad children are…

_____

_____

_____

Lonely children are…

_____

_____

_____

_____

Angry children are…

_____

_____

_____

_____

Session 2: Pals' Training Year 6

Aims

To break down barriers within the group.

To teach the group how to approach, talk to and encourage another child.

To teach the group how to respond appropriately to other children.

To teach the importance of eye contact.

To raise the children's self-esteem.

Resources

Good Things About Me activity sheet.

Teacher's notes

Game

Fruit Cake is a fun game to relax the group, break down inhibitions and prepare them for the rest of the session.

Round

I find this the quickest and most practical way of discussing their playground observations. It is useful to note down any observed behaviour that you think might be problematic for the Pals to deal with so that this can be discussed and role-played when discussing problems in Session 3.

Pair-work

This section will provide further insight into what is happening on the playground and possibly provide some problems to discuss in Session 3.

Skills

Listening, empathy, body language.

Game

I'm Passing My Smile

This is most effective when played in the circle as the eye contact and non-eye contact are dramatically different. Hopefully they will understand that eye contact is important to establish trust and for a person to believe that you are interested in what they are saying.

Rounds

Something I'm pleased with myself about

You need to model this for the children and give them some examples, such as, 'I'm pleased with myself that I helped my mum with the washing up, that I tried hard in maths, that I'm in the football team.' Someone may still say something like, 'I'm pleased that I'm going on holiday,' if so, gently ask them what they have done that they are proud of, as the idea behind this exercise is to help build the children's self-esteem by encouraging them to think positively about themselves.

Something nice about the person on my left

Again this is a difficult one for most children and you will probably need to give them some examples, such as, I like your shoes, I think you are good at football. I find it useful to make the analogy between receiving a compliment and receiving a present, hence saying thank you. Hopefully they won't need reminding about eye contact.

Discussion

How did it feel?

Anticipated answers are shown in brackets. By getting the children to reflect on how they felt, it is probable that they will make the connection that they may help some unhappy children to feel better about themselves by saying something nice to them. It is worth mentioning that an angry child on the playground may react negatively to anything nice being said or done to them. Help the group to relate to this by asking them about how they feel when they are in a temper or cross. Make the point that sometimes children and adults need to calm down before they can have a conversation. This will be dealt with in greater depth in the next session.

Role-play

For the role-play, demonstrate a poor way of making contact, for example, run across the room to the child shouting hello, then make eye contact asking them a string of questions without waiting for an answer, then look away and pretend to have a conversation with someone else and without looking back at the child say, 'I'll be back later,' and go!

Ask the pupils what was bad about your approach. They should come up with the right answers and usually find this very amusing.

Then ask for a volunteer to model the right way. Ask the pupils what they think was good.

It is intended that the children understand and practise the following, which you hopefully elicit from them by the suggested question and your role-play demonstration:

▸ A gentle approach with a friendly smile and eye contact, trust and esteem building statements and questions, such as:

'Hello my name is…, what is yours? That's a nice name.'

'Whose class are you in? What is your friend called?'

▸ An understanding of whether the person is ready to be helped (check their body language) or not and how to respond appropriately:

'Can I come back in five minutes?' Or: 'I'll come back in five minutes,' and keep an eye on them from a distance.

▸ Helping the child play with her own age group and not become dependent on the Pal. The Pal needs to help the children organise a game, join in or watch for a couple of minutes and then leave, letting them know they will be back to see how they are getting on in a little while.

If they don't think of the above (they usually do) then use any of the suggested questions to tease additional information out of them:

▸ What have we learnt about listening, body language, eye contact, etc. that will help us to help children on the playground?

▸ Why is it not a good idea to run up to someone who may need your help?

▸ What would their body language tell you about how they are feeling when you approach them?

▸ What do you think you should say first of all?

▸ When you've started speaking to them, what would tell you that they were open to you?

▸ What would tell you that they were not ready to chat and be helped?

▸ What could you do then?

▸ Is it a good idea to stay with them for the whole of play? Why?

When the children are practising their role-plays, it is helpful if you move around from pair to pair with some encouraging suggestions to keep them on task! If you are able to have a classroom assistant or lunch-time supervisor with you, it is useful to have another adult to help with this. Don't worry at this stage about how they deal with problems in their role-plays, as this will be dealt with in the following sessions. You may like to allow time for the children to show each other their role-plays and reflect back some constructive criticism.

Game

Changing Object

This serves to reinforce esteem building in others and the response, 'No, but good try,' could be discussed, as to how it helps let people down gently and encourages them to have another go.

Preparation for next session

A healthy self-esteem is essential for our social and academic growth and development and I think this is a good opportunity to build the self-esteem of the Pals by helping them to focus on and memorise something positive about themselves.

Timing

If you are short on time, spend less time on the first and last game and omit the showing of the role-plays to the group.

Activities

Game

Fruitcake

A child is chosen to have the first go.

The others then ask questions, such as, 'What football team do you support?' to which the player is only allowed to answer, 'Fruitcake,' without laughing or smiling.

As soon as they laugh or smile, the child who asked that question is then 'it'.

Round

One sentence comment on task from Session 1. Encourage the children to say something that hasn't been said if possible.

'What I noticed on the playground was...'

Pair work

In pairs the children have two minutes to agree on:

'One thing we enjoy about playtime...'

'One thing we dislike about playtime...'

Go round the circle and each member of the pair completes each question respectively.

Ask them if they think that other children like or dislike the same things as them. Thinking about these things and what they observed on the playground, how could the Pals help to improve the playground?

(Hopefully you will get suggestions such as teach them games, play with them, help them sort out problems.)

Skills

Ask the group what skills were discussed in the last session that would be helpful for a Pal to have.

Explain that this week you will consider the importance of eye contact and helping others feel good about themselves.

Game

I'm Passing My Smile

Model this for the group by choosing the pupil on your left, making eye contact, saying, 'I'm passing my smile to X,' and smiling at the child. This child then says, 'Thank you,' returning the eye contact and turns to pass the smile on to the person on their left.

One round is made with eye contact, one round with each person looking at the ground as they pass their smile.

Ask the children:

▸ Which version is better and why?

▸ Why do you think eye contact is important if you are trying to help a child?

Rounds

Something I'm pleased with myself about.

Something nice about the person on the left.

Explain that we need to receive a compliment (something nice someone says about us) as if we were receiving a present: receive it and say, 'Thank you!'

Discussion

Ask the group:

How does it feel to say something nice about myself? Another person? (Awkward, embarrassed, good, happy.)

Make the point that it takes seven positive comments for us to believe one of them, whereas we believe one negative one straight away.

Ask the group: How could you help children on the playground to feel happier about themselves? (Introduce into the initial conversation a compliment, such as, 'I like your shoes,' or, 'That's a nice name.')

Role-play

Ask for a volunteer and role-play, in turn, a bad and good approach to a child on the playground. Ask for the pupils' comments on each one respectively.

In pairs the pupils take it in turns to play the Pal with their partner being the child needing help.

Game

Changing Object

Choose any object, for example, a ruler.
Mime using it as a comb, wand or pencil, etc. (Just choose one mime.)
The children have to guess what it is being used as.
Whoever guesses correctly has the next go.

Jenny Mosley adapts this in her book *Quality Circle Time in the Primary Classroom* to include the phrases, 'Well done,' if someone guesses correctly and, 'No, but good try,' if the guess is incorrect. This is a good way of teaching the children to be positive with one another and to encourage those who might feel bad about getting something wrong.

Rounds

'One skill I learnt from this session is…'

Preparation for next session

Hand out the Good Things About Me activity sheet and explain that the Pals have to be positive about themselves and bring the sheet to the next training session.

Good Things About Me

Write and illustrate some good things about you.

For example: I help my friend with her work. I am helpful.

_____

_____

_____

_____

_____

Differentiation Guidelines Year 2

Game

Fruitcake is a fun game to relax the group, break down inhibitions and prepare them for the rest of the session. You will need to provide them with some examples of questions.

Skills

You will need to explain what skills are: What a Playground Pal does to make them a good Pal is perhaps a good option, asking them to tell you what they learnt last session.

Games

I'm Passing My Smile

It is helpful to repeat this game with everyone looking at the floor, to enable them to understand through experience the importance of eye contact. Ask them what is nicer, someone passing them a smile and looking at the floor, or someone looking at them?

Rounds

Something I'm pleased with myself about.

Something nice about the person on my left.

This would be fine to leave out if you feel that there are enough new ideas for your group to take in this session and introduce it in the next session.

Preparation for next session

Hand out the Good Things About Me activity sheet and explain the task.

Good Things About Me

Complete the following sentences.
You can draw as well if you want to.

I am good at...

_____

_____

_____

_____

My friends like me because...

_____

_____

_____

_____

At school I really like...

_____

_____

_____

_____

Session 3: Pals' Training Year 6

Aims

To raise the children's self-esteem and enable them to raise the self-esteem of others.

To increase the children's understanding and ability to deal with different emotions.

To problem-solve potential difficulties they may encounter as Pals.

To teach basic assertiveness and anger management skills.

To explore conflict resolution.

Resources

Role-plays.

Teacher's notes

Game

Cowboy, Freeze!

Cowboy, Freeze! needs to be fast moving and fun! The idea is to break down inhibitions and gel the group together ready for the rest of the session.

Good things about me

The idea is to help the children build and reinforce positive views of themselves. Where possible ensure pairings are safe and conducive to this. It is useful for yourself and another adult to wander round and check that they have understood the exercise and encourage them. You may like to finish this exercise with a quick round:

'One good thing about me is...'

Ask the children how they could use the exercise they have just done to help a child on the playground.

'One game I could teach other children is...'

Ask the group to have several in mind so as not to duplicate when going round the circle. You could use the time at the end of the session to play a couple of suggested games (children's choice).

Possible difficulties

I've listed some of those that usually occur but you may have others particular to your school. It is helpful to list these difficulties down for everyone to see. I've included possible solutions that the group might come up with for a quick reference. You may like to write the problems out and pair the children up to discuss and feed back solutions or do it as a group.

It is helpful to try and elicit problems and solutions from the children, as where there is some ownership, they will be more likely to remember them.

It is also useful to ask the children to provide you with examples: 'What would a child who wanted to be boss all the time be like to play with?' and 'What might they be doing in a game?'

You will need to define what you mean by bully and decide how much responsibility you want the Pals to take with regard to bullying behaviour. Remind them of the school rules about bullying.

Children who want to be boss all the time

Explain to them that they need to take it in turns with others in choosing games, etc. Find another child willing to play with them and monitor while they take turns in choosing and playing a game.

Children who don't know how to share or take turns

Involve them in games where there is a lot of turn-taking and sharing.

(Naming games, Cowboy, Freeze!, Follow the Leader, Fruit Salad – keep changing the leader, Changing Object....)

Children who don't know any other children to play with

Build up their confidence by having a chat. Play a game with them and gradually involve other children. Leave them in the middle of a game and tell them you'll be back to see them in a few minutes.

Children who are bullies

Tell an adult. If you have been assigned a particular child to monitor, involve them in sharing and turn-taking games.

Children who are being bullied

Tell a teacher. Take them away from the situation.

Children who don't want to talk to the Pal, who run off or are aggressive

Try again in five minutes. Don't take it personally, they are not upset with you. If they still don't want to talk tell an adult and note their name and your concern down in the book.

Children teasing and name-calling other children and Pals

For Pals to do and help others to do: Don't take it personally. Walk away. Tell an adult.

Fights

Get an adult and keep other children away.

Some of the solutions will vary from school to school. In cases of fighting, name-calling and bullying, you may wish the Pals to report straight to a teacher or LTS.

Help them to work through some solutions by careful questions such as:

▸ What games could we play to teach children how to share, take turns etc.?

▸ How could we help a child who:
  likes to be boss all the time?
  has no friends?
  is shy, aggressive or runs off?

When you come to name-calling, don't mention Mr Friend at this stage, but take down their suggestions, because it is important for them to see that you value them and they may have some brilliant suggestions. You can ask them at the end of the session what problems they think Mr Friend would be helpful for solving.

Mr Friend

The idea of this section is to teach basic assertive skills and requires a lot of adult input. Name-calling and wind-ups are popular problems. The groups always take this section seriously and the feedback is always very positive. I have never been short of a volunteer to share a name that they get called, but, if no one volunteers, pick a volunteer and role-play calling them a name. Make sure it is not a name they could ever have been called, e.g, pick someone who does not wear glasses, give them a pair of sunglasses and call them 'four-eyes'. Alternatively, tell them to call you 'four-eyes' and you wear the glasses.

It is important to make the point that the idea is not to call back a name or even say something that is similar to name-calling, for example, 'Well at least I've got a mum,' as a retort to an insult about her mother.

The children seem to relate well to the concepts of unkind words or names being deleted from a computer screen and a best friend sticking up for them. For those who can't, help them to remember a time when someone stood up for them, or encourage them to imagine what you, as a supportive adult, would say on their behalf. For any children experiencing emotional or behavioural difficulties, or who regularly have a problem with how they respond to name-calling and wind-ups, encourage them to remember a time when they responded inappropriately and let them re-enact that situation out with an appropriate response. If this is too difficult for them, let their partner model the appropriate reaction first and then let them have a go. Further practice on these kind of issues can be done in the additional training sessions.

Special mention needs to be made to the tendency in a lot of schools for children to insult one another's families. In my experience, this can quickly erupt into a fight, in some instances the mere mention of the words, 'Your,' or, 'Your Mum,' is enough to evoke a violent reaction from the victim. I think this taunt is so successful in provoking a reaction because it is linked to the basic security and identity of the child and, in many cases, the accusation is linked to the hurt of rejection. (Especially if the child is from a single parent family or doesn't know their father or mother.) If this is a problem in the school, I deal with it by ensuring that each child has an opportunity to address this during the paired role-play. Some of the group may need extra coaching and encouraging or the support of the other Pals in order to deal with this appropriately when on the playground, if they are there because they experience emotional and behaviour difficulties and this is a particular problem for them. Similarly, if this is not a problem in your school, then it might be better not to mention it, unless it arises at a later stage. The idea is not to create new versions of name-calling.

Discussion

The idea is that the children appreciate the difference between being assertive and aggressive.

Rhyme

This is something I have found useful to teach the children who have problems with name-calling.

I often make the analogy with a buzzing wasp: the more you show that you are scared and the more fuss you make, the more the wasp tries to hang around you, whereas if you keep calm and ignore it, it will go away.

You could develop this as literacy and citizenship work and incorporate rhymes and pictures with a display about bullying and the playground.

Skills

Games, problem-solving, assertiveness, self-esteem raising.

By now the children should be well used to analysing skills they have learnt.

Game

It may be an idea to play one or more of the earlier suggested games, especially if any are new to you or the group. It would be useful for the Pals to practise explaining the games to each other, so ask for volunteers, or let the children who originally suggested the game introduce it to the group. If you have a lot of new games, you could split the group into two, so more children get the opportunity to have a go.

Rounds

A skill I learnt in this session is…

Preparation for the next session

A list of suggested scenarios can be photocopied and distributed to the Pals. Alternatively the children can create their own, to last two or three minutes, illustrating the type of situations they may encounter as Pals and how they would deal with them.

Activities

Game

Cowboy, Freeze!

The leader calls out whatever they want the others to mime, for example, 'Cowboys.'

When the leader calls 'Freeze!', everyone holds still. Encourage the children to take it in turns to be leader.

Some further examples are policeman, fireman, elephants, mice, teachers, children, gardeners, swimmers or walking the dog.

Paired activity

Read Good Things About Me to each other.
Test each other on how many you can remember.

Rounds

Note down the games the children suggest and if they are unknown to the majority, allow some time at the beginning or end of the sessions to play them. Where possible encourage the children to avoid repetition.

Discuss and brainstorm

Possible difficulties they may encounter as Pals.

Suggested question: Remembering Sami and Sasha from Session 1 (re-read the stories if necessary) and your playground observations, what problems might you come across on the playground?

Solutions

Go through each problem trying to elicit solutions from the children either as a group or if you have more time put them in pairs or small groups to discuss solutions and then feed back.

Role-play: Mr Friend

Explain that you are going to teach them another way of dealing with name-calling.

What would a best friend do or say if they were with you when you were being called names?

(Hopefully you will elicit that a good friend would stick up for you and say something nice to comfort you.)

Explain the following:

I want you to imagine that inside your head lives Mr Friend. Whenever anyone says any unkind words or calls you names, Mr Friend deletes the unkind words from the computer screen inside your head and writes out kind words about you for you to speak out and think about.

It is useful if you model the above by selecting a pupil to call you a name and you demonstrate how to respond. I've included some examples for you to use if you need to.

Examples

Name	Answer
Carrot-top	'My hair is a lovely colour and a lot of people pay a lot of money to dye their hair this colour.'
Fatty	'I'm not fat I'm just right,' or, 'We're all different, it would be boring if we were all the same.'
Four-eyes	'That's not true – I've got two eyes and a great pair of glasses.'
Your mum's smelly	'That's not true,' or, 'You don't know my mum.'

(Please refer to teacher's notes.)

Ask for volunteers to be called a name by you.

Depending on the group, you may well have some children who are willing to make themselves vulnerable and share names they have been called or those that are common on the playground.

It is a good idea if you start off by doing the name-calling and reinforce the fact that this is a role-play exercise and you don't mean it.

Pair practice

The children choose someone in the group and practise calling each other names and responding assertively. It is helpful to have another adult with you for this session to enable you to successfully monitor this exercise and check that the children have understood the principles involved.

Discussion

How did you feel? (Hopefully you will elicit comments such as, 'I felt strong inside, it felt good.')

Ask them how this could be useful to a Pal?

Rhymes

Introduce the idea that sometimes it is useful to have a rhyme to share or think about.

> One example is the following:
> Keep cool as ice, think of something nice,
> It will go away.
> Get in a flap, call a name back
> And it will stay.

You may like to set the children an additional task of creating some of their own rhymes and pictures to go with a Playground Display or for use in assembly.

Rounds

A skill that I learnt from this session is…

Game

Children's choice (see teacher's notes).

Preparation for next session

Put the children into groups.
Distribute the role-plays activity sheet. Ask them to find some time to practise their role-play before the next training session.

Role-plays

A new pupil is standing alone on the playground looking sad and lost.

(Show this by body language.)

Show how you would help.

Remember:
- How will you go up to them?
- What will you say?
- How will you help them?

Characters:
- Pal
- pupil
- friends.

Two friends have fallen out, they come up to you both saying each has called the other nasty names and they don't want to play together any more.

How would you help them sort this out?

Remember:
- listening
- eye contact
- how to put it right.

Characters:
- Pal
- pupils.

A child is upset and crying because some children have been calling him names.

How would you help?

Remember:
- Calm them down.
- Help them feel better with kind words.
- Mr Friend.

Characters:
- Pal
- pupil.

Differentiation Guidelines Year 2

One game I could teach other children

These will be somewhat different from what a Year 6 group would suggest.

Discuss and brainstorm

Possible difficulties they may encounter as Pals.

It would be better to keep this discussion in a group.

Role-play

If the children find it difficult to grasp the idea of Mr Friend, an alternative is to ask them to practice the phrase, 'I like you, but I don't like it when you… (call me names), please stop.'

Preparation for next session

If the role-play is too complex for the ability of the group, the How I Can Help activity sheet could be substituted.

How I Can Help

Draw and write what you could do as a Pal to help:

A new pupil is standing alone in the playground.

_____

_____

_____

_____

Two friends are calling each other nasty names.

_____

_____

_____

_____

A child is crying because other children are name calling.

_____

_____

_____

_____

A child is spoiling a game by cheating.

_____

_____

_____

_____

Session 4: Pals' Training Year 6

Aims

To raise the group's self-esteem.

To build the group's confidence and ability to deal with problems on the playground.

To revise all we have covered in the training sessions.

To discuss an assembly to introduce the Pals to the school.

Resources

Small bag of sweets or pieces of fruit.

Pal Guide booklet, folded and stapled. It would be good if this could be photocopied onto coloured card to make it look good, as the better the preparation, the more important the Pals will feel.

Pal Certificate, to be photocopied onto card and given out in assembly.

Teacher's notes

Game

If you decide to use the Grandma's Box, you can reinforce the language of self-esteem by the phrases, 'No, but good try,' and, 'Yes, well done.'

Rounds

Model this for the children and give them some examples:

'I like your shoes, I think you are good at...'

'You were kind to me when...'

Allow a minute's silence, while everybody thinks about their positive statement.

Role-plays

Encourage the children to use constructive criticism after each sketch by responding to questions such as: 'Which skills that we've learnt did you see used in the sketch?'

Taunting

This taunting example is only necessary to mention if you think it appropriate for your school situation.

Pal Guide Booklets

The eight pages for the Year 6 Pal Guide Booklet are on pages 60-63 and must be printed onto two double sided pages of A4 paper. The two pages of A4 will then be folded in half to make an A5 size booklet. Pages 60-63 are laid out in such a way that, when the pages are folded in half, the booklet pages will be in the correct sequence.

Pages 60 and 61 must be printed back to back on the first page of A4 paper and pages 62 and 63 must be printed back to back on the second. Then place the first page on top of the second page and fold in half so that the bottom half of page 60 forms the booklet front cover and the top half of page 60 forms the booklet back cover. The excess paper can then be trimmed to the edge of the booklet.

There are spaces left for the children to add their own ideas.

Encourage the children to identify any of their ideas included in the guide. This encourages ownership and makes them feel important.

The suggested assembly (p58) could be used alongside the children's sketches to provide further examples of the kind of situations they will be helping with. You may wish to incorporate some rhymes as mentioned in Session 3.

Reflection

This is only supposed to help them reflect on something that they have learnt today. There will be further opportunity for evaluation and reflection in the follow-up session.

Game

Try and ensure that each Pal has by this time had a go at introducing and leading a game. If you have additional time, you could pair up those who have not yet introduced a game and let them practise explaining a game and allow a minute or so of play.

Follow-up session

Depending on the size and type of group, you may wish to have this after one, two or three weeks. If you think that the children will need to have additional support to cope with the rota sooner rather than later, then organise the follow-up session soon to allow for more Pals to be trained more quickly.

Activities

Game

Grandma's Box

Grandma's Box is an imaginary box, which you mime taking something out of which the group have to guess; whoever guesses correctly gets to mime next. Ask for volunteers to introduce and lead the games.

Rounds: Something positive about my neighbour

Remind the group about the need to receive compliments.

Explain that they are going to say something nice about the person on their right, who, as before, will say, 'Thank you.' After the round, pass everyone a sweet or piece of fruit, and, as they eat, encourage them to think about the positive comment.

This is not as absurd as you may think and actually helps the children to focus on the positive comment; they quite enjoy the food as well!

Role-play

The group perform and evaluate their role-plays. You may wish to give them a few minutes practise prior to showing them.

Discuss

Any further problems they may have thought of.

Ask, 'How would you deal with persistent taunting of a child by a group of children or another child?'

You may wish to practise 'The Mr Friend response' again.

Or ask if anyone has had any success with handling teasing.

Distribute and discuss

Distribute the Pal Guide Booklet which summarises all you have done so far.

Ask if they have any questions.

Here would be a good place to mention the book used to record any incidents, that is if you decide to have one, what is appropriate to record and what is not.

Also, discuss the use of play equipment if you decide to have it and possible dividing of the playground, so that there is one area reserved for games with the Pals or use of skipping ropes and other play materials.

Assembly

Gather ideas from the children. If you want to you can use the suggested assembly below.

Assembly idea

Three children are playing a clapping game.
Two of them gang up on the third, saying,
'You're cheating, we're not going to play with you any more.'
The child responds, 'That's not fair, I wasn't cheating.'
The others reply, 'Yes you were,' and walk away.
The child is upset. 'Who shall I play with now?'

Children freeze and drum roll. (If you like!)
Enter Pals. (In uniform, larger than life gestures.)
Pal 1: 'Do you sometimes have no one to play with?'
Pal 2: 'Do you sometimes fall out with your friends?'
Pal 3: 'Don't worry, we're the Playground Pals and we're here to help.'

Rap: If you're ever on the playground feeling sad,
         Don't have a long face, don't you feel bad,
         Just around the corner are some friends for you,
         We're called the Playground Pals, so don't be blue.
Repeat the above two or three times. Children freeze.

It may be a good idea at this point for the teacher to introduce the Pals making the following points.

▶ How they will be recognised.
   This is something that most of Year 6 will have the opportunity to be involved in.

▶ Pals are only available to be played with when on duty. (This is particularly for the infants who tend to mob their favourite Pal whether or not they are on duty!)

- This is an important befriending role within the school to help make playtimes happier for everyone and any children who tease the Pals will have their names written in a book and be seen by a teacher. (This is particularly for those juniors who may tease the Pals.)

- Clarification of boundaries, e.g. what Pals will be doing, what they won't be doing.

- You may like to include the role-plays from Session 4 as examples of the kind of situations the Pals may be helping with.

Reflection round

One skill I've learnt today is…

Game

Children's choice

Follow the same format as for the start of the session.

Follow-up session

Reinforce that they will be put on a rota and will trial as Playground Pals for two weeks and then have a follow-up session to evaluate how they have been getting on and discuss training some more Pals.

· ·

Have fun and thank you

Playground Pals

Name

▸ A child who does not want to be helped – accept this, but come back in five minutes to try again, if this does not work, tell a teacher.

▸ Anger and name-calling towards you. Keep calm! Do not take this personally, it is their problem. Walk away or think about what a best friend would say to comfort you. Tell a teacher or supervisor or note it down in the book so that a teacher can deal with it at a later date.

▸ Help! Something I can't cope with! We stay calm and go and tell an adult.

▸ Name-calling. Explain what you learnt about Mr Friend.

▸ Others:

_____

_____

_____

_____

Possible Problems!

Fold along dotted line

Playground Pals

Games

To teach turn-taking, sharing, letting others be boss, winning and loosing.

Skipping, cards, Chinese-whispers, catch, Zip-Zap, Fruitcake, What's the Time Mr Wolf?, Hopscotch, name games, Stuck in the Mud, There is a Space on my Right, Duck Duck Goose, changing object, Cowboy, Freeze!, Farmer's in his Den, Grandma's Box, clapping games, running games, Oranges and Lemons and Ring-a-ring-a-roses.

Others:

_____

_____

Remember how it feels and looks to be left out and upset

Sami felt angry, confused and hurt. He looked angry and cross.
Sasha felt sad and unwanted. She looked scared and lonely.

How you can help

Introduce yourself and smile! Listen well! Make eye - contact.
Ask their name and say something to make them feel happy, such as,
'That's a nice name,' or 'I like your shoes...'

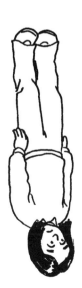

If they are happy to chat

Ask them about themselves (favourite television programme, colour etc.) to help them relax and trust you.
Then ask, 'What's wrong? Can I help?'

If they are negative towards you

Say: 'I can see that you are upset, would you like to talk about it?' or
'I'll come back in a few minutes and see if you'd like to chat then.'

When you have found them someone to play with

Suggest a game and play it with them, make sure they understand the rules.
Remember the games that teach children how to be fair, take turns.
When you need to go, explain that you will be back to check they are OK later.
It is important that you do not play with them all the time.
The idea is to help them to play with children of their own age group.

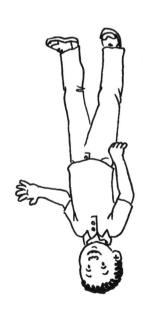
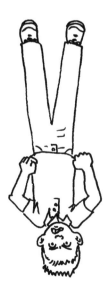

Playground Pals

Congratulations!

Name: .... Date: ....

Has completed a training course and is now a

~ Playground Pal ~

Signed: ....

Differentiation Guidelines Year 2

Game

Grandma's Box

This can be difficult for infants, both to guess and to demonstrate. It might be more appropriate to substitute one of their suggested games from the previous session, or to use Fruit Salad or a variation.

Fruit Salad and Postman are different versions of the same game. Go around the circle and give each child a piece of fruit or a number, for example, apple, pear, banana, apple, pear, banana, or one, two, three etc. When you call a particular fruit or fruits they must stand up and change places. If you call Fruit Salad, everyone changes places. Similarly, with numbers, those numbers that you call change places and when you call Postman, everyone changes places.

Round

Something positive about my neighbour

If you left this out in Session 2, give them some examples of the kind of compliments they can give:

'I like your shoes…', 'I think you are good at…'

'You were kind to me when…'

Allow a minute's silence, while everyone thinks about their positive statement.

Discuss

Are there any further problems they may have thought of?

Distribute and discuss

Pal Guide Booklet, which summarises all you have done so far.

These have been adjusted to differentiate for infants.

The eight pages for the Year 2 Pal Guide Booklet are on pages 67-70 and must be printed onto two double sided pages of A4 paper. The two pages of A4 will then be folded in half to make an A5 size booklet. Pages 67-70 are laid out in such a way that, when the pages are folded in half, the booklet pages will be in the correct sequence.

Pages 67 and 68 must be printed back to back on the first page of A4 paper and pages 69 and 70 must be printed back to back on the second. Then place the first page on top of the second page and fold in half so that the bottom half of page 67 forms the booklet front cover and the top half of page 67 forms the booklet back cover. The excess paper can then be trimmed to the edge of the booklet.

For those that find reading difficult you could highlight with a pen the points that you consider most important for them to remember. They may need reassuring that you do not expect them to perfectly remember everything in the booklet, make the point that it is like a dictionary, they don't need to carry it on the playground with them!

Allow a minute's silence while everyone thinks about their positive statement.

Assembly

You will probably need more time to practice the assembly. Use the same as Year 6. (See Page 58)

The suggested assembly could be used alongside the children's sketches to provide further examples of the kind of situations they will be helping with. You may wish to incorporate some rhymes as mentioned in Session 3.

Reflection

This is only supposed to help them reflect on something that they have learnt today. There will be further opportunity for evaluation and reflection in the follow-up session.

Game

Try and ensure that each Pal has by this time had a go at introducing or leading a game. If you have additional time, you could pair up those who have not yet introduced a game and let them practice explaining a game and allow a minute or so of play.

Follow-up session

Depending on the size and type of group, you may wish to have this after one, two or three weeks. If you think that the children will need to have additional support to cope with the rota sooner rather than later, then organise the follow-up session sooner to allow for more Pals to be trained more quickly.

Have fun and thank you

Playground Pals

Name

Fold along dotted line

- If a child does not want to be helped – go away, but come back in five minutes. If this does not work, get help from an adult.
- If somebody calls you a nasty name, keep calm and go and get help from an adult.
- Help! Something I can't cope with! Stay calm and go and get help from an adult.
- Others:

_____

_____

_____

_____

_____

_____

Possible Problems!

Playground Pals

Games

To teach turn-taking, sharing, letting others be boss, winning and loosing.

Skipping, cards, Chinese-whispers, catch, Zip-Zap, Fruitcake, What's the Time Mr Wolf?, Hopscotch, name games, Stuck in the Mud, There is a Space on my Right, Duck Duck Goose, changing object, Cowboy, Freeze!, Farmer's in his Den, Grandma's Box, clapping games, running games, Oranges and Lemons and Ring-a-ring-a-roses.

Others:

_____

_____

Remember how it feels and looks to be left out or upset
How you can help

Introduce yourself and smile! Listen well! Make eye contact.
Ask their name and say something to make them feel happy, such as,
'That's a nice name. I like your shoes…'
If they are happy to chat
Ask them about themselves.
Then ask what's wrong. Ask if you can help.
If they are not friendly towards you
Say: 'I'll come back in a few minutes and see if you'd like to chat then.'
When you have found them someone to play with
Play a game with them.
When you need to go, explain that you will be back to check they are OK later.
It is important that you do not play with them all the time.

Playground Pals

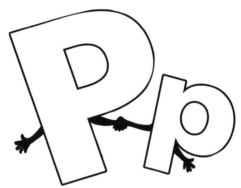

Congratulations!

Name: .... Date: ....

Has completed a training course and is now a

~ Playground Pal ~

Signed: ....

Follow-up Sessions and Additional Training

▸ The idea of this session is to give the opportunity for a structured evaluation of what is working well for the Pals and what they are finding difficult. It is hoped that this will be a positive session and solution focused in approach, looking at what they are enjoying and doing well and praising them for it and, from that standpoint, looking at the few teething problems.

▸ It is important to be supportive and explain at the onset that it is natural to have a few difficulties, they are learning: but it is also important to allow them to problem-solve any difficulties. Resist the urge to solve it for them! Usually there are few difficulties and when explored further, the Pal has already solved it, or can describe a time they coped with it.

▸ I envisaged that once the scheme is up and running there could be fortnightly follow-up sessions run along the lines of Circle Time. I have also included three more slightly more focused training sessions, which are designed to extend the Pal's skillbase. If you find fortnightly follow-up sessions difficult to fit in, then try it once every half term, but do try and check regularly that everything is OK, even if it's a brief visit to the Year 6 classroom. Some follow-up sessions could be self-managed with a different Pal or two running the session and feeding back to you. The on-going success of this scheme depends upon your on-going enthusiasm and commitment to it.

As for the other training sessions, seat the children in a circle, if possible on chairs.

Game

Children's choice

Let them choose by voting on their favourite game.

Rounds

What is good about being a Pal?

What is difficult about being a Pal?

It is helpful if the teacher records the comments as an aid to future training of Pals.

Problem-solve

(If you have recorded the problems on a white board, you can refer to them and ask how they would solve them.)

The difficulties are usually connected to lack of respect for or teasing the Pals and infant mobbing when the Pals are not on duty. It is helpful to discuss these and the underlying issues such as jealousy, Pals needing to practice assertiveness, etc. Schools usually iron these out in assembly and include rules such as the following:

▸ Being a Playground Pal is an important job, which most children will have an opportunity to do in Year 6. Anyone teasing or taunting the Pals will be seen by a teacher.

▸ Infants cannot go up to a Pal if they are not on duty (not applicable for Year 2).

Discussion

Which of the skills that they've learnt have they found particularly helpful to their work as Pals?

(Listening, eye contact, body-language, empathy, self-esteem raising, communication, problem-solving, playground games, anger management, self-confidence.)

Planning the next training sessions

The following may be helpful to consider with the children, it is very important to give them as much ownership as possible of the training. Included are examples I have found helpful, but you may have better ones.

▸ How to choose/select the new Pals.

▸ What aspects of our training shall we include?

▸ Who will do the training? How will we do it?

It is not necessary to replicate the exact format of the training if you don't have the time. Once you have one group of Pals trained, they can become a resource to help teach the next groups. It could take the format of two thirty minute sessions in two consecutive lunch-times, depending on how quickly you want to get the new Pals trained.

Session 1

Pair an existing Pal with one or two new ones and have them run through each of the skills explaining and modelling them. Have them also explain any of the problem-solving suggestions and practise Mr Friend.

Session 2

Depending on the size of the group, split into smaller groups of ten and let the Pals take it in turns to teach the games.

▸ Do we send the trainees out on the playground with a current Pal? This has been very successful in schools.

▸ Organisation of new rotas.

Your original Pals may be 'Pal-ed out' if there are only a few and they have been on duty a lot. Find out if any need a breather and organise the rota to accommodate this after their initial training session with a new Pal on the playground.

Assembly

If the profile of the scheme needs raising, then do a similar assembly with all the Pals.

Recording incidents

Some schools adopt the system of a book, usually left at reception or in the Year 6 classroom, in which the Pals can record any difficulties. This can be checked daily (or as often as possible) by you and any appropriate action taken.

It is important to clarify again what kind of things can be recorded and what is not acceptable. E.g. Telling tales, being unkind are not acceptable.

Noting down a particular child who might have been very upset, or a child who is often alone, may be the kind of things you wish to include.

Use and abuse of play equipment

Depending on what system or not you have in place, you may need to explain this.

Lunch-time supervisors

You may wish to include a lunch-time supervisor who can feed back positively any issues arising from their standpoint.

Additional training

You may want to offer some extra training to the Pals to improve their skills in listening, mediation and anger management. These short sessions are only intended to improve their roles as Pals and are not meant to turn them into trained mediators.

Listening

Resources

picture
feeling cards
blank paper and pencils
seat everyone including you in a circle.

Game

Chinese Whispers

You may like to play this twice.

Make the point that we listen best when we really want to hear what is being said.

We are going to do some activities that will help us to practise listening.

Change places if you have... blue eyes, a dog, etc.

Go round the circle and let everyone take a turn at making up a reason to change places.

Picture game

Distribute paper, something to rest on and pencil.

Explain that you will tell them a story and that when you stop and say 'picture' you want them to make a picture in their heads and then very quickly draw it. It doesn't have to be best drawing. It may be an idea to get them to divide their paper into four and draw one picture in each quarter.

One day Ellie the elephant was bored and decided to go and explore the jungle where she lived. It was a sunny day and the birds were singing as she set off.

Picture 🗀

She hadn't gone very far when she came across Monkey.

'Hello, what are you doing?' asked Monkey.

'I'm going exploring,' replied Ellie.

'Can I come?' asked Monkey.

'Of course,' said Ellie. 'Climb aboard.'

So Monkey climbed up and sat on Ellie's head.

Picture

They hadn't gone very far when they came across Bird.

'Hello, what are you doing?' asked Bird.

'We're going exploring,' they said.

'Can I come?' asked Bird.

'Of course,' they said. 'Climb aboard.'

So Bird hopped up and sat on Monkey's shoulder.

Picture

They had a great day exploring and by the bedtime they were all very sleepy as they said good-bye. Ellie got home and raised her trunk into the sky and made a happy sound.

Picture

Using their pictures as prompts, ask for volunteers to tell different segments of the story back to you. Ask them if having the pictures helped them remember better?

Explain that one way of helping you to listen to what someone is saying is to make pictures in your head of some of the things they are telling you about.

Pair work

Explain that they are going to practice listening to each other. Go round the circle and pair them up, labelling them A and B. Explain that they might not be with someone that they know very well, but that this is good practice for being a Pal.

Ask that A's tell B's what they like to do when they are not in school. B's are to remember at least two things and be able to tell the group.

Swap them after a couple of minutes. Each partner introduces the other to the group and says as much as they can remember.

This is… and she likes watching television, playing football and playing with her dog.

Discuss

Was that easy? Difficult? Why?

Reflective listening

Explain that we can help others to know that we are listening to them and understand what they are saying by telling them how we think they are feeling.

Using the sheet How Are They Feeling, discuss how Pals could respond.

If someone is telling you something and they seem sad, by the way they are standing and how they are speaking, you can say:

You look (or sound) sad, what would help make you happy?

In the same way, if they are angry say:

You look (or sound) angry, what would help make it better?

If they are upset say:

You look (or sound) upset, what would help you feel better?

Using the sentence, 'I haven't got anyone to play with,' model saying it in an angry, sad and then upset manner respectively. On each occasion ask for volunteers to practice reflecting back how they think you are feeling.

Game

Partner, You Look...

Each pupil is given a Feelings Card (that they don't show anyone) and, in turn, mimes the feeling word written on the card. The person to the left says, 'Partner, you look...' (whatever they think they are miming). If they get it right the partner says, 'Yep, I'm feeling...' and it is then the partner's go. If she gets it wrong, the new partner says, 'No, no, have another go,' and chooses a different pupil. If no one has guessed after three attempts, the partner says the feeling word they are thinking of. The game continues round the circle until everyone has had a go.

Does anyone have any particular difficulties with listening?

Rounds

I need to listen more when…

Simon Says

Go round the circle and let everyone take a turn at leading for a couple of sentences.

Feelings Cards

Angry	Happy
Sad	Frustrated
Irritated	Scared
Lonely	Lost
Fed-up	Unhappy
Cross	Upset

How Are They Feeling?

Mediation

Resources

Helpful Hints sheet (yr 6 & yr 2)
picture sheet
picture cards.

Teacher's notes

Seat everyone including yourself on chairs in a circle.

Explain that we are going to think about mediation.

Ask if anyone knows what 'mediation' means.

Mediation is another word for helping people sort out difficulties they may be having with each other. So we are going to look some more at how we can help children to do this.

Round (Spider!)

Go round the circle and say the first word you think of when I say, 'Spider!'

Hopefully you will get varied responses as to some a spider is a delight and they may well be into Spider Man, whereas others might be a bit more squeamish in their response.

Make the point that people look at things in different ways.

Picture examples
Picture 1

A lot of arguments and upsets start because people look at things differently.

Look at this picture. You might be really good at skipping or football and hope to be chosen for the team and so want to practice as much as possible and want to play it with your friend. Your friend might be really bad at skipping or football and feel embarrassed and not want to play. If you don't understand each other you could end up falling out.

In arguments people waste time and energy on attacking each other with words.

Often the problem is forgotten.

Picture 2

In this picture the children both want the same reading book. What would be better than arguing about it?

Hopefully they will say something along the lines of talking about how to sort it out so that both children are happy.

Explain that this can be called a win-win situation, with both children happy at the end.

Picture 1

Look at this picture again. Two children have fallen out because they both want to play different games.

What would you do first as a Pal?

Hopefully they will say calm them down and listen to each side in turn.

What would you do next?

Hopefully they will say ask how to make it better.

Role-plays

Put the children in threes. Tell them that two of them will pretend to be the children who have fallen out about something on the playground and the third will be the Pal.

Pal is to ask: 'How are you feeling?'

                'What would make it better?'

(They may need to prompt younger ones with feeling words, such as happy, sad, angry, upset.)

Provide them with the following examples: (Show them picture 1 to provide a focus for each example.)

▸ Two children have fallen out over a game. They both play it in a different way and have slightly different rules but they don't understand this.

▸ One child accidentally bumped into another and made them spill their crisps. They have ended up calling each other names.

Ask them if they can think of any other conflict situations they have come across on the playground, they may like to use these. (You can wander round and check on the role-plays as they are practicing them.)

Ask them to present their role-plays and comment on them.

Assertiveness game

Explain that a useful phrase to teach children to stand up for themselves is:

'I like you, but I don't like it when you…, please stop or I will get help from a teacher/adult.'

Using the picture cards, ask for a volunteer to take a card and using the picture, make up an example of something one child might do to another in the classroom or on the playground, for example, a picture of a pencil. A child might take someone's pencil without asking to borrow it. Ask for a volunteer to show how they would answer this using the above phrase. If the person successfully answers they get to choose someone to have a go who hasn't yet had one.

Helpful Hints prompt sheet

Hand out and discuss.

The traffic light is a useful symbol for them to remember. (Simpler version for Year 2.)

Red   Problem alert! Listen to the facts and feelings.
Amber What would make it better?
Green Action, do it.

Picture Examples

Picture 1

Picture 2

Helpful Hints

Do's

Do help those who ask for it.

Do help with friendship problems.

Do help with teasing and name-calling.

Do listen carefully to each side of the story. What's the matter?

Do ask questions to show that you understand. You look or sound unhappy/angry/sad/down. How do you feel?

Do ask for suggestions? What would you like to happen? What would make things better?

Don'ts

Don't mediate an argument while it is going on.

Don't take sides.

Useful phrase: I like you, but I don't like it when you . . . . Please stop, or I will get a teacher.

Listen – facts and feelings.

Suggestions – What would make it better?

Action – A solution that works for everybody.

Helpful Hints

Useful phrase:

I like you, but I don't like it when you

. . . .

Please stop, or I will get a teacher.

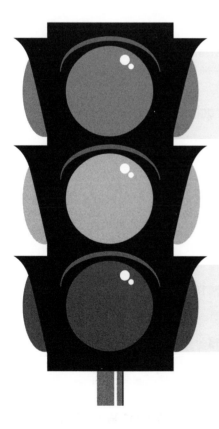

Listen to the person.

Idea – think how to make it better.

Action – a solution that works for everybody.

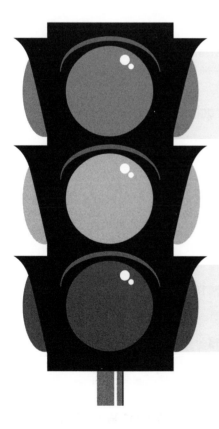

Year 2

Picture Cards

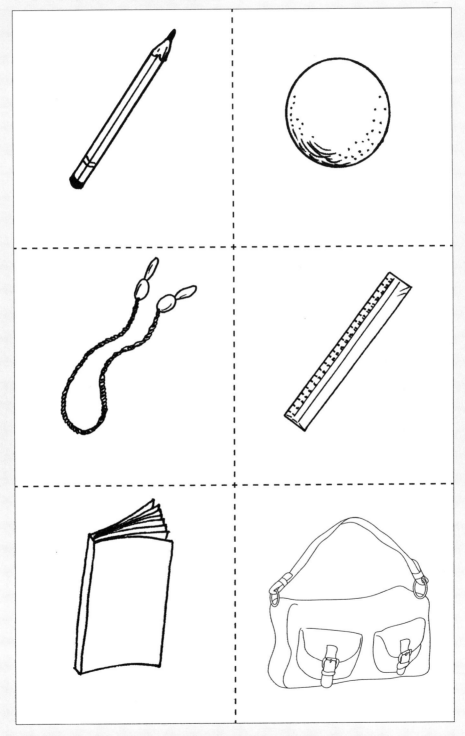

Anger Management

Resources

The Angry Picture.
Plain paper, pencils, crayons.
Seat everyone including you in a circle on chairs.

Game

Cowboy, Freeze!

This is played the same way as before, but emotions are used as well, for example, angry children, happy people and sad people.

Look at the picture. How do you think this person is feeling (angry)?
Why might they be feeling angry?

Round

I feel angry when...

We all do different things when we feel angry.
When I feel angry, I sometimes...

Explain that anger is not wrong, it is a feeling like being happy or sad. What we do with our anger can be wrong.

Pair work

Draw a combined picture of what your anger might look like, such as a monster. Draw or write on one side things that will make the anger bigger (more angry) and things that will make the anger smaller (less angry).

Bigger: shouting at someone or hitting someone,

Smaller: relaxing, calming down and trying to sort it out when you are calm. Thinking about something else, going for a walk.

Feed back with the group and discuss: How could this help us as Pals?

Rounds

'When I get angry, I could make my anger monster smaller by…'

Game: Children's choice.

The Angry Picture

Lunch-time Supervisors (LTSs)

Introduction

LTSs have a challenging role as they supervise young people at an unstructured part of the day and have a much higher child/adult ratio.

The following are some of my observations collected over the years of the situation for LTSs within schools.

▸ It is generally accepted that implicit in any teacher training course will be behaviour management techniques, which will be fine-tuned over the years with classroom experience and In Service training. Whereas, many lunch-time supervisors may well have received no formal training in managing challenging pupil behaviour.

▸ There are usually more behaviour problems at lunch-times.

▸ Lunch-time supervisors may well have a low profile within the school and are not respected in the same way as teachers by pupils and parents/carers.

▸ They may feel like 'second class citizens' within the school community.

▸ There can be a 'them and us' culture between the LTSs and teachers.

▸ Channels of communication between LTSs and teachers are often poor.

▸ LTSs may have little or no knowledge of the school behaviour policy.

The following is a suggested four session training course that informs the lunch-time supervisors about the Playground Pals scheme and seeks to address some of the above problems.

Sessions 1 and 2 cover the Pals training,
Session 3 discusses a questionnaire relating to their work and
Session 4 can be adapted to the needs of your particular school.

Any work undertaken with LTSs will undoubtedly impact the other areas of the playground system. Often, training of LTSs gives rise to a larger staff meeting and opens up wider discussions relating to school life.

▸ It is important that they get paid for the extra two hours, both to validate what they are learning and to raise their own profile of themselves.

▸ Where possible try to elicit the information you require from them, as people are far more likely to practice something they feel they have some ownership of.

- It is helpful if you can provide coffee and biscuits at least for the initial session as this sets the tone and helps create a relaxed, non-threatening environment.

- You will need to adapt the sessions accordingly in line with the Year 2 sessions (please refer to Year 2 amendments if you have trained Year 2 Pals).

Session 1: LTS Training

Resources

Tea, coffee, biscuits, Playground Observation sheets, Good Thoughts About Me sheets and Pal's Guide book.

▸ Explain the aim of the scheme is to train pupils to identify and intervene with low level playground behaviour problems and that it is hoped that the Pals will lighten the supervisor's work load by reducing the amount of incidents they are responsible for.

▸ They may well be nervous. Your expertise as a positive, non-threatening facilitator may well be required. Depending upon the situation in your particular school, they may need to know that you are on their side as it were, not the expert, but the facilitator.

▸ Explain that you will run through the main elements of the scheme; today's session covering highlights of the first two training sessions that the Pals have had and next weeks covering the last two. Their last two sessions will be more personally relevant for their work..

▸ It is important that you get them to sit in a circle.

▸ Run through the following highlights from sessions 1 and 2 of the Pals training. I've selected those activities that I think most helpful, but by all means take what you think will be helpful from the sessions. (The games and activities will work their usual magic of breaking down barriers and helping everyone to feel comfortable together.) Each session is written as it would be for the children's training to help you to remember it, you will obviously change the presentation to make it more appropriate for adults.

Part One

Guidelines for explaining Session 1 of the Pal's training to the LTSs

Start by explaining the aims of the session for the Pals.
Play both of the name games briefly.
Explain the rules.
Play the listening games and do the rounds.
Explain the game, Space on my Right. There is no need to play it.
Briefly explain the rest of the session and play Zip Zap.

Playground Pals Training: Session 1

Aims

To break down barriers and inhibitions within the group.

To help the group appreciate the feelings of those with whom they will be working.

To develop listening skills and show the importance of listening.

To establish a safe working framework for the group through rule making.

To help the group to be aware of different types of body language.

Name games

My name is and this is...

Sally calling Harry, Harry calling Mike.

Rules

Explain that it is necessary to create some rules to ensure that everyone feels safe and happy in the group.

Suggested rules

We listen when someone else is speaking.

We may pass.

What we say in the group stays within the group.

There are no put downs, only put ups!

Listening games

Ask group to describe non-listening behaviour.

Put them into pairs – A and B.

A's start by telling B's what they like to do out of school, B's do not listen. A's and B's then swap roles. (Allow about two minutes for each conversation.)

Go around the circle allowing each person the opportunity to complete the sentence, 'When I'm not listened to I feel...'

Repeat the previous game, but this time each partner should take a turn demonstrating listening behaviour.

Rounds

'When I'm listened to I feel...'

'Why are good listening skills essential? (To help the children feel that they matter, that you are really interested in what they have to say and are helping them.)

Game: There is a Space on my Right...

To highlight the importance of including everyone.

Round

'A time when I felt left out was...'

How do we identify pupils who need the help of Playground Pals?

Body language is sad, angry or lonely.

Acting out or acting in behaviour.

Discuss how Pals will be recognised, for example, by wearing sweatshirt, bands etc.

Preparation for next session

Research what is happening on the playground.

Game: Zip Zap

Give them the Playground Observation sheet and explain you'll discuss later this session what the results are.

Part Two

Guidelines for explaining Session 2 of the Pal's training to the LTSs

Explain the aims.

Play Fruitcake.

Discuss the results from the task.

Play the game I'm Passing My Smile and do rounds and discussion.

Explain role-play and round.

It is a useful exercise to give the supervisors the Good Thoughts About Me activity sheet to complete as we can all do with raising our self-esteem. I also find it helpful to provide them with a copy of the Pal Guide Book for reference, so they can see exactly what the children have learnt.

Playground Pals Training: Session 2

Aims

To break down barriers within the group.

To teach the group how to approach, talk to and encourage another child.

To teach the group how to respond appropriately to other children.

To teach the importance of eye contact.

To raise the children's self-esteem.

Game: Fruitcake

Round

Discuss the results from the Playground Observation sheet. Does anything about the Pals' comments surprise them?

Game: I'm Passing My Smile

To teach the importance of eye contact.

Which version is better and why? Why do you think eye contact is important if you are trying to help a child?

Round

Something I'm pleased with myself about.

Something nice about the person on the left.

'I like your shoes, hair, your handwriting, your football playing,' etc.

Explain that we need to be able to receive a compliment (something nice someone says about us) as if we were receiving a present – receive it and say, 'Thank you!'

Discuss

How does it feel to say something nice about myself? Another person? How could you help children on the playground to feel happier about themselves? (Introduce into the initial conversation a compliment such as, 'I like your shoes, that's a nice name.')

Role-play

How we could use all the above to approach and start talking to a child.

Round

One skill I learnt from this session.

Preparation for next session.

Hand out Good Things About Me sheet.

See activity sheets at the end of Playground Pals Year 6 Session 1.

Session 2: LTS Training

Resources

Pal booklets (if not distributed in Session 1).

Questionnaire.

Part One

Guidelines for explaining Session 3 of the Pals' training to the LTSs

Welcome the group and reiterate that you will continue with the highlights from the final two training sessions for the Pals.

Play Cowboy, Freeze!.

Paired exercise Good Things About Me and ask for their comments. Did they find it easy? Why?

Run through any games the children suggested and ask if the LTSs have any others.

Ask if they can foresee any problems the Pals might encounter.

Run through the problems, solutions and Mr Friend.

Explain the rhyme.

Playground Pals' Training: Session 3

Aims

To raise the children's self-esteem and enable them to raise the self-esteem of others.

To increase the children's understanding and ability to deal with different emotions.

To problem-solve potential difficulties they may encounter as Pals.

To teach basic assertiveness and anger management skills.

Game: Cowboy, Freeze!

Paired activity

Read Good Things About Me to each other.

Test each other on how many you can remember.

Round

'One game I could teach other children is…'

Discuss and brainstorm

Possible difficulties they may encounter as Pals and solutions.

Have the supervisors any suggestions? Refer to problems and solutions mentioned in Session 3.

Mr Friend (Dealing with name-calling.)

What would a best friend do or say if they were with you when you were being called names?

Examples

Carrot-top

Answer: 'My hair is a lovely colour and a lot of people pay money to dye their hair this colour.'

Fatty

Answer: 'I'm not fat I'm just right.' 'We're all different and I'm OK.'

Four-eyes

Answer: 'That's not true. I've got two eyes and a great pair of glasses.'

Your mum's smelly

Answer: 'That's not true,' or, 'You don't know my mum.'

Rhymes

Sometimes it's useful to have a rhyme to share or think about.

Keep cool as ice, think of something nice,
It will go away.
Get in a flap, call a name back
And it will stay.

Part Two

Guidelines for explaining Session 4 of the Pal's training to the LTSs

Play Changing Object.

Do the Compliment a Neighbour exercise.

Explain the purpose of the role-plays.

Distribute Pal Guide Booklet.

Mention assembly.

Ask for their comments on the training.

Playground Pals' Training: Session 4

Aims

To raise the group's self-esteem.

To build the group's confidence and ability to deal with problems on the playground.

To revise all we have covered in the training sessions.

To discuss an assembly to introduce the Pals to the school.

Game

Changing Object or one or two of their suggested playground games. Ask for volunteers to introduce or lead the games.

Round

Something positive about my neighbour.

Remind the group about the need to receive compliments.

Explain that they are going to say something nice about the person on their right, who, as before, will say thank you. After the round, pass everyone a sweet or piece of fruit and as they eat, encourage them to think about the positive comment.

Role-play

The group perform and evaluate their role-plays. (Obviously this is for reference only; the midday supervisors do not have to do role-plays.)

Distribute and discuss

Hand out the Pal Guide Booklet which summarises all you have done so far.

Ask if they have any questions.

Here would be a good place to mention the book used to record any incidents (that is if you decide to have one), what is appropriate to record and what is not.

Also to discuss use of play equipment if you decide to have it and possible dividing of the playground, so that there is one area reserved for games with the Pals or use of skipping ropes and other play materials.

Assembly

Gather ideas from the children. If you want to you can use the suggested Assembly on page 58.

Evaluation round

'One skill I've learnt today is ...'

Explain about the follow-up session and additional training.

Hand out the LTS questionnaire. This is to be completed then discussed informally at the next session. Explain it is not an attempt to catch them out, but to serve as a helpful assessment of their needs, skills and expectations with regard to their work.

Lunch-time Supervisor's Survey

1. What do you like about your job?

_____

_____

2. What do you dislike about your job?

_____

_____

3. Do you think the pupils respect you? Why?

_____

_____

4. What are the most difficult aspects of your job?

_____

_____

5. Do you feel supported in your job? By whom?

_____

_____

6. Do you think you have a high profile within the school? Why?

_____

_____

7. How do you discipline children?

_____

_____

8. How do you reward children?

_____

_____

9. Is this linked into the school behaviour policy?

_____

_____

10. What would make your job easier?

_____

_____

Session 3: LTS Training

Resources

Behaviour Management notes.

Round

What I like about my job.

Discussion

Survey

Work your way through the questions on the survey and explain that you will note down any important factors that arise from the discussion. You will know what particular issues need to be addressed in your school and the discussion in this session provides an excellent forum for you to introduce the particular points you want to raise. It goes without saying that issues need to be addressed with gentleness and diplomacy.

I usually make the following points:

▸ The low ration of adults to children at lunch-time.

▸ They manage a difficult job superbly.

▸ Their lack of training in behaviour management compared to a teacher.

Give out the Behaviour Management points and discuss them. I always make the point that these are things I'm constantly having to remind myself of, for example, trying to establish control by not shouting and provide them with an example of the last time that I blew it. Keep the examples brief. This is to help communicate to them that you're not approaching them as the 'expert' and to make them more amenable to taking on new ideas.

Where possible try to elicit the information from them. The more they feel that they own the points that arise from the discussion, the more likely they will be to practise them.

I suggest that I type up the points arising from the discussion for them, which serves to give some significance to what they have said and also to remind them of any points that you may have wanted them to take note of. I have included a sample, which you may like to adapt. It is good if you can acknowledge them on the sheet. End the session by thanking them for their time and input.

Behaviour Management

(A sample of the kind of behaviour issues raised during training)

▸ Two children come up to you telling tales about each other. Listen to each in turn, acknowledge their feelings by use of, 'Mmm, I understand.'

'You look or sound angry or sad, what would make you feel better?'

'You've told me nasty things about each other, can you tell me something nice about each other?'

'What could you do to sort this out?'

▸ Try not to shout, it loses children's respect. Are you being assertive, aggressive or passive? Are you reacting to the child's behaviour or responding to it?

▸ Knowing the rules, rewards and sanctions will help you to be more confident. Always refer to these when speaking to a child. Try and be consistent with rewards or sanctions, that's why it is so important to have an agreed set of rules that everyone follows, so you know what behaviour to reward/praise

▸ Praise – catch children doing it right and praise them, for example, 'Well done Sammy, you've picked up your rubbish.'

▸ For inappropriate behaviour – label the act not the child.

'I'm surprised that such a kind boy would hit Joe. What could you do to put it right?'

▸ For defiant or confrontational children, try humour to de-escalate the situation if appropriate.

For example, 'You're great at being cross – you should be in the school play. Can you show me being friendly?'

If not, use the language of choice to provide them with the sense of some control.

For example, 'You can choose to do what I've asked, or you can choose to… (go inside, whatever reprimand ties in with school system.)'

▸ The broken record technique simply involves repeating your instruction and not being drawn into secondary issues.

For example, 'I can understand you feel angry at having to go in, and we can talk about that when you've calmed down, but right now I'd like you to go and stand by the wall.'

It has been suggested that there be a whole-staff meeting to:

1. Discuss behaviour policy for break-times.

2. Devise a set of lunch-time rules for the playground and classroom and children's involvement.

3. Discuss buying lunch-time play equipment.

4. Discuss raising profile of school support staff.

5. Agree whole-staff approach to common behaviour difficulties. Further training needed.

6. Whole-staff mission statement on how to promote positive behaviour.

Some solutions to the above that have worked in practice

1. Reward stickers for positive behaviour as outlined in school rules. LTSs given receipt book to issue congratulatory note to child and a copy given to class teacher. If a child gets three in a half term a praise letter goes home informing parents of their exemplary playground behaviour. In a similar way, using a different colour receipt as part of a hierarchical sanction system for breaking rules, such as warning, followed by two minutes against the wall, followed by a slip and if a pupil gets three slips a term their parents/carers are invited in to discuss the inappropriate behaviour.

2. Lunch-time rules devised with class and all support assistants during a teacher led Circle Time session. Rules gathered and selected for use by whole school.

3. Playtime equipment such as skipping ropes, balls, hopscotch, giant jacks, bought and monitored in a zoned area of the playground.

4. LTSs assigned to a specific class for a term. Photo of LTS, support assistants and class teacher on notice board with names. LTS introduced to class at beginning of term, attend class assembly, class trips, end of term party. Pop in once a week in agreement with teacher.

5/6. Training on how to promote positive behaviour summed up by developing a mission statement.

Session 4: LTS Training

Resources

Games to play.

Round

'What I have found most helpful about the sessions so far is...'

Games to play

Distribute and read through, ask for comments. Do they play with the children or just organise and supervise which games they find work the best?

Role-play

Explain that you think it would be helpful to do a bit of improvisation.

They will have examples of situations that they find difficult to handle.

They can pair up and show the way they might have dealt with it and how they will deal with it now: e.g. utilising a prepared script, broken record, assertive manner.

If they are happy to they can show each other and discuss. If not, you can ask them to feed back how they will deal differently with a situation and what they have learnt.

Here are some scenarios:

How to deal with:

A defiant child and practising the broken record.

A child who says, 'I don't have to listen to you, you're only a midday supervisor.'

A child who wants you to get involved in secondary issues.

Practising making the child responsible for their behaviour.

Key phrases:

'The rule is....'

'You can choose to... or you can choose...'

Round

Something I've learnt from these training sessions.

Present them with their certificates.

Following on from these sessions, it may be appropriate to develop certain issues further.

Games to play

Duck, Duck, Goose

Children stand in a circle, one caller child walks around outside of circle and gently touches back of each child in turn saying Duck, Duck, etc. When he or she says 'Goose' the goose child chases him around the outside of the circle. If the Goose successfully catches the caller before the caller reaches the Gooses' place, then the caller repeats the process. If the caller reaches the place without being caught, the Goose becomes the caller.

What's the time Mr Wolf?

'Mr Wolf' stands with his or her back to a line of children about 5 or 6 metres away. The children chorus, 'What's the time Mr Wolf?' who answers, 'Two o' clock,' etc. and the children take that number of steps forward. This continues until Mr Wolf says, 'Dinner time!' and catches the new Wolf.

The Farmer's in his Den

The children stand in a circle with the farmer in the middle. They chant the following, with each appropriate character choosing the next one mentioned, until the bone is chosen and they all pat the bone. The bone is now the new farmer.

> The farmer's in the den, the farmer's in the den. Eee ii iddly ii, the farmer's in the den.

Repeat above using the following phrases. The farmer needs a wife, The wife needs a child, The child needs a dog, The dog needs a bone, We all pat the bone.

Oranges and Lemons

Two children form an archway with their arms, through which all the others must pass. Everyone chants:

Oranges and lemons, say the bells of St. Clements. You owe me five farthings, says the bells of St. Martins. When will you pay me, says the bells of old Bailey.

When I grow rich, says the bells of Shoreditch. When will that be, says the little bell of Lea. I do not know, says the great bell of Bow.

At which point the children move the arch up and down as each child passes through saying, 'Here comes a chopper to chop off your head, chip chop chip chop the last man's dead.' At this point the child who is between the arch joins on behind one of the children who is part of the arch.

Chinese Whispers

The children stand in a circle. The leader chooses a phrase or word like 'fish and chips' and whispers it to the child on his or her right without the others hearing. This is then passed round the circle. When the last child has listened to it, he or she speaks it out!

Ring-a-ring-a-roses

The children stand in a circle and chant the following, falling down at the end!

'Ring-a-ring-a-roses. A pocket full of poseys. A tissue, a tissue. We all fall down.

Tip

Set them up in a game that will meet their individual needs or encourage a Pal to do so.

Provide a verbal hug by the use of words such as 'I'm going to leave you to play, but I'll be thinking about you.'

Playground Pals

Congratulations!

Name: .... Date: ....

Has completed a training course for
Lunch-time Supervisors

Signed: ....

Appendix

Draft letter for Year 6 parents/carers

Dear Parent/Carer

Your child . . . . has been selected to undergo training to become a Playground Pal. This is a new scheme, which we would like to use in school to help all children enjoy happy playtimes.

The four 30 minute training sessions, will take place in school hours and will enable your child to successfully recognise and help children on the playground who may not have anyone to play with or know any games to play. It is anticipated that the Pals will be on duty at playtime every other week for one day. The training is available to most Year 6 pupils who would like to participate and I regard it as an excellent opportunity for them to develop citizenship skills and responsibility in preparation for secondary school and in line with the National Curriculum.

Should you have any questions about the training, please contact me. Unless I hear otherwise, I will assume that you have no objection to . . . . participating in this scheme.

Yours Sincerely,

Draft letter for Year 2 parents/carers

Dear Parent/Carer

Your child . . . . has been selected to undergo training to become a Playground Pal. This is a new scheme, which we would like to use in school to help all children enjoy happy playtimes.

The four 30 minute training sessions, will take place in school hours and will enable your child to successfully recognise and help children on the playground who may not have anyone to play with or know any games to play. It is anticipated that the Pals will be on duty at playtime every other week for one day.

The training is available to most Year 2 pupils who would like to participate and I regard it as an excellent opportunity for them to develop citizenship and social skills in line with the National Curriculum.

Should you have any questions about the training, please contact me. Unless I hear otherwise, I will assume that you have no objection to . . . . participating in this scheme.

Yours Sincerely,

Sample Information Sheet

Playground Pals

In a letter format addressed to the Head or teacher responsible for training, explain why you think you would make a good Playground Pal.

You may illustrate it.

The following points may give you some idea of what to put in your letter.

I think I would be a good Playground Pal because…

> I have been an infant monitor.

> I have been a reading partner.

> I like helping people.

> I know a lot of younger pupils.

> I'm kind and I enjoy playing with all sorts of people.

> I make up good games.

> If there was an argument I would listen to both sides of the story.

> I am used to playing with and helping younger children as I have younger brothers, sisters, cousins.

> I would be committed and not go off and play with my friends.

> I am friendly.

> I am helpful.

> I am responsible.

Year 6

Playground Pals

Use some of the following to help you to make up some sentences and pictures to explain why you think you would make a good Playground Pal.

Give your words and pictures to (insert name of teacher).

I think I would be a good Playground Pal because…

  I like helping people.

  I know a lot of younger pupils.

  I'm kind and I enjoy playing with all sorts of people.

  I make up good games.

  I am used to playing with and helping younger children.

  I am friendly.

  I am helpful.

Year 2

Important News
for all Year 6 Pupils

....
....

Playground Pals

Do you like helping others?

Do you want us to have happier play?

Would you like to be a leader?

If the answer is Yes to any of these questions, you could take part in training to become a Playground Pal in school this term. Tell .... if you are interested.

Teacher Survey Part 1

1. Are lunch-time playtimes more difficult than mid-morning playtime?

   _____

   Why? _____

   _____

   _____

2. Are lunch-time meals a problem in the school?

   _____

   Why? _____

   _____

   _____

3. What do you think would help the lunch-time supervisors in their job?

   _____

   _____

   _____

4. How do you think the children and staff view the lunch-time supervisors?
   Staff: _____

   _____

   _____

   Children: _____

   _____

   _____

5. Do you think the lunch-time supervisors should have some formal training in Behaviour Management?

   _____

   Why? _____

   _____

   _____

Teacher Survey Part 2

6. What are they good at?

_____

_____

_____

7. In what areas could they receive more support?

_____

_____

_____

8. How do you resolve discipline problems that have arisen on the playground?

_____

_____

_____

9. What do you perceive to be the main problems encountered by children on the playground?

_____

_____

_____

_____

_____

Pupil's Survey Part 1

1. Do you think the lunch-time supervisors do a good job?

   _____

   Why? _____

   _____

   _____

2. Do you think their job is difficult?

   _____

   Why? _____

   _____

   _____

3. Do you think any children are lonely or upset at playtime?

   _____

   Why? _____

   _____

   _____

4. What kind of problems do children have at playtime?

   _____

   _____

   _____

5. Are there any lunch-time rules? What are they?

   _____

   _____

   _____

6. Do all the children know them?

   _____

   _____

Pupil's Survey Part 2

7. What happens if you are naughty at lunch-time?

8. What happens if you are naughty at playtime?

9. Do the lunch-time supervisors play games with children and talk to them?

10. Do they discuss naughty children with the teachers?

11. What do you like about playtime?

12. What do you dislike about playtime?

Letter to Parents/Carers and Governors

Dear Parent, Carer and Governor

We are currently researching our playground and break-time needs and would appreciate any comments or observations you may have under the following headings.

Space

_____

_____

Appearance of play area

_____

_____

Activities

_____

_____

Pupil relationships

_____

_____

Supervision of children

_____

_____

Any others:

_____

_____

_____

_____

Supervisor's Survey

We are currently researching our playground and lunch-times and would appreciate your comments.

1. What is the best thing about supervising meals?

   _____

   _____

   _____

2. What is the worst thing about supervising meals?

   _____

   _____

   _____

3. What could be done to improve mealtime?

   _____

   _____

   _____

4. What is the best thing about lunch-time (excluding the above comments)?

   _____

   _____

   _____

5. What is the biggest problem you face?

   _____

   _____

   _____

6. What could be done to improve lunch-time?

   _____

   _____

   _____

Bibliography

Barnes, P. (1995) *Personal, Social and Educational Development of Children,* Open University.

Bateson, P.P.G.(1976) *Discontinuity in development and changes in the organisation of the play of cats.* In K. Immelmann, G. et al. Behavioural Development, London: Cambridge University Press.

Blatchford, P. and Sharp, S. (1994) *Breaktime and the School: Understanding and Changing Playground Behaviour,* London: Routledge.

Blatchford, P. and Sumpner, C. (1998) *What do we know about breaktime?* Brit. Ed. Research Journal, 24, 1, 79-94.

Bliss, Robinson and Maines (1995) *Developing Circle Time,* Lucky Duck Publishing.

Brewer, D. (2000) *Lunch Matters.*

Cowie, H. and Sharpe, S. (1996) *Peer Counselling in Schools – A time to listen,* London: Fulton.

Cowie, H. and Sharpe, S. (1996) *Peer Support Forum: Principles of Good Practice In Peer Suport Projects.* www.mentalhealth.org.uk/peer/forum.htm

Peer Support Report: Executive Summary (2002) The Mental Health Foundation.

Curry, M. and Bromfield, C. (1994) *PSE for Primary Schools through Circle Time,* Nasen.

DfEE 0112/2001 *Promoting Children's Mental Health within Early Years and School Settings.*

DfES (2003) *Tackling Bullying: Listening to the views of children and Young People* – Summary Report.

DfES (2000) (2002) *Bullying: Don't Suffer in Silence.*

Headstart – East London *100 Games and activities for the school playground,* Learning Design.

Lawrance, D. (1988) *Enhancing Self-esteem in the classroom,* Paul Chapman Publishing Ltd.

Long, R. (1999) *Making sense of behaviour: The art of self-esteem,* NASEN.

Mcnamara, S. and Moreton, G. (1995) *Changing Behaviour,* David Fulton Publishers.

Mosley, J. (1996) *Quality Circle Time in the Primary Classroom,* LDA.

National Healthy Schools Standard: www.wiredforhealth.gov.uk

Naylor, P. and Cowie, H. (2000) *Peer Support Challenges Bullying in Schools,* University of Surrey Roehampton: Princes Trust.

Pellegrini, A.D. and Blatchford, P. (2000) *The child at school: Interactions with peers and teachers,* New York: Oxford University Press.

Pellegrini, A.D. and Blatchford, P. (2002) *Time for a break: the developmental and educational significance of breaktime in school.* The Psychologist, 15, 2 60-62.

Pollard, A. (1996) *The social world of children's learning,* Cassell.

Scroufe, Cooper, Dehart (1988) *Child Development,* McGraw Hill.

Smith, Charlie (2002) *Best Buddies,* Lucky Duck Publishing.

Smith, P. and Cowie, Helen (1996) *Understanding Children's Minds,* Blackwell.

Stacey, H. and Robinson, P. (1997) *Lets Mediate!* Lucky Duck Publishing.

Vygotsky, L. (1978) *Mind in Society,* Cambridge, M.A. Harvard University Press.